Acknowledgments

I should like to acknowledge my special indebtedness to Mr Michael Buckby of the Language Teaching Centre, University of York and late organiser of the Schools Council French Project.

I should also like to thank Mr Anthony Howatt of the Department of Linguistics, University of Edinburgh, Mr David Harding of the Department of Education, University of Leeds, and Mr Jim Simpson of the Schools Council for their comments on various chapters in this book.

Finally, I would like to acknowledge the help of the following M.A. students in the Department of Education at Leeds, who managed to read the more tortuous sections of this book during their teaching practice and who gave me help in the refining of my ideas: Sister Caroline, Mrs Shirley Emmins, Mr John Fogelman, Mr Robert Llewellyn, Mr Peter Metcalfe, Miss Pat Pattison.

We are grateful to the following for permission to reproduce copyright material:

Edward Arnold (Publishers) Ltd., for *Répétitions* by Ventners and King, artist C. King, (Fig. 12); Amateur Swimming Association, Loughborough, for poster No. 3 of 3 entitled 'Survival Swimming' issued by Bovril Ltd., for the A.S.A. (Fig. 28); The British Council for 'The Use of Pictures by Language Teachers' in *Educational Development International* October 1974, by Andrew Wright, (Fig. 65); Dorothy Cloynes (Fig. 25 left hand page, top and middle right); The Cognitive Research Trust for *The Dog-Exercising Machine* by Edward de Bono, (Fig. 36); J.M. Dent & Sons Ltd., and Doubleday & Co. Ltd., for Sketches from *Brain Boosters* by David Webster, copyright © 1964, 1965, 1966 by The American Museum of Natural History, (Fig. 29); Mary Glasgow Publications Ltd., for German Cartoons and *Entrechaux*, (Figs. 32 and 47); Arthur Guinness Son & Co. Ltd., for 'The Guinness Pipeline' advertisement, (Fig. 31); George G. Harrap & Co. Ltd., for *Die Eisenbahn-Serie* No. 4 by I. Meyer, (Fig. 72) and *Deutsch in Bild und Wort* by K. Jewry, (Fig. 84); Keystone Press Agency Ltd. (Fig. 25 left hand page, middle left); Language Materials Development Unit, University of York, for *Faites Vos Jeux* by M. Buckby and D. Grant, (Fig. 9) and Macmillan Education for *Kaleidoscope*, 1A (Fig. 76) and 1B (Figs. 75, 78); Longman Group Ltd., for *First Things First*, by L.G. Alexander (Figs. 39, 86), *Topical Research Workbooks*, Book 1 Looking Around by D. Boothman et al, (Figs. 34, 50), *What Do*

You Think? Book 2 by D. Byrne and A. Wright, (Fig. 35), *Impact Assignments in English* by R.B. Heath, (Fig. 30), *Longman Audio-Visual French Course* A3 (Fig. 87) and B3 (Fig. 16), *Language Teaching Analysis* by W.F. Mackey, (Fig. 11), *SCOPE, English for Immigrants Project*, Stage 1 Picture Book, (Fig. 22); *Mad magazine*, © 1968 by E.C. Publications Inc., cartoon, (Fig. 33); Nuffield Foundation for *En Avant* Stage 2, (Figs. 64, 70, 79), Stage 4A, (Figs. 20, 74) and Stage 4B (Figs. 19, 37, 51); Oxford Delegacy of Local Examinations, for GCE Summer 1971 O-level French, Paper 1, Oral 2, (Figs, 45, 46); Oxford University Press for 'Language Without Words' in *ELT Journal*, XX No. 3 by M. West, © Oxford University Press 1966, (Fig. 88); Royal National Life Boat Institution for poster No. 2 of 4 entitled 'How the Life Boat Service Works' issued by Duckhams Ltd., for the R.N.L.I., (Fig. 63); The Schools Council and E.J. Arnold & Son Ltd., for *A Votre Avis*, (Figs. 4, 81) and *Dans le Vent* magazines 7 and 8 (Figs 71, 80); Yorkshire Evening Press (Fig. 2 and Fig. 25 right hand page, top right).

Illustrations by Andrew Wright: Fig. 1, 3-10, 13-15, 17, 18, 20-24, 26, 27, 37, 38, 40-44, 48, 49, 52-62, 64-70, 72, 73, 76, 77, 79, 81-83, 85, 89-135.

Note The majority of these illustrations were drawn specifically for this book. They are very simply drawn in order to provide a model for the teacher's own manufacture of materials.

Longman Handbooks for Language Teachers
General Editor: Donn Byrne

Visual Materials for the Language Teacher

Andrew Wright

Longman

LONGMAN GROUP LIMITED
London

*Associated companies, branches and representatives
throughout the world*

©Longman Group Ltd. 1976

First published 1976
Reprinted 1979

ISBN 0 582 52267 6

Printed in Hong Kong by
Wilture Enterprises (International) Ltd

Preface

For many years visuals have been judged mainly, even solely, by their ability to aid comprehension unambiguously. People have earnestly taken pictures produced for language teaching and subjected them to interpretation tests. 'Do the interpretations tally with the text associated with the pictures in the course^' Some pictures are pronounced successful language teaching pictures; others are condemned. Certain language items, it is said, as a result of these tests, should never be taught by means of the visual; other types of language 'lend themselves to visualisation'.

There are many occasions when it *is* helpful if the picture or pictures are unambiguous. However, I feel very strongly that the emphasis in talking about visual materials and language teaching should not be placed solely on the evaluation of pictures related to their lack of ambiguity.

Firstly, visual materials have *many* roles to play in language learning. The roles are quite different and the forms of the appropriate visual materials are equally varied. Secondly, a grasp of the meaning of an item in the foreign language is unlikely to occur at any *one* moment in time, either in conjunction with a picture or with mother tongue equivalents.

There are many aspects to the meaning of the simplest of words; a sense of these meanings can only be built up by experiencing each item in a variety of contexts. And language is not just single words, but groups of words, whose association and relationship conveys meaning. Semantic meaning and formal meaning, are complex and not usually picked up in any significant way at the drop of a hat.

In any case, the first grasp of the meaning of a new item is, as every teacher knows, merely the first step of a long and stony way to a firm grasp of meaning and an ability to use that language item productively.

Visual materials are a source of help *throughout* this long process, as I hope will be made convincingly clear in the following chapters.

A.W.

Contents

PART TWO: Media

PART THREE: The perception of visual materials

PART FOUR: How to do it

Further reading

Appendices

PART ONE: Visual materials and language learning

Introduction

Many media and many styles of visual presentation are useful to the language learner. There is no general rule to indicate which medium and which visual style are appropriate at any one time.
The choice is affected by :

- the age, interests, type of intelligence and experience of the student;
- the physical circumstances of the classroom or laboratory;
- the cost and convenience of the materials available.

The teacher's own experience will help him to judge the relevance of these points.

The chapters in Part One emphasise the importance of two further factors. The use of visual materials to help create situations:

1 which interest the pupil
2 in which verbal communication would be a natural element to a native speaker (intrinsic language) and not an act artificially prefabricated and imposed by the teacher.

The traditional divisions of Part One are for general convenience only. What really matters is the specific use or uses of each visual at any one time. The more precisely one can say what the visual material is to contribute in a particular situation the more likely one is to be able to choose and use the media available effectively.

1 Listening

The use of visual materials for listening activities.
There are three sections in this chapter.

Teaching the meaning of new items

Listening discrimination

Extensive and intensive listening

Many of the points made on the use of visual materials in the teaching of meaning could have been equally well made in the chapter on reading. However, for convenience, the entire discussion of this aspect of language teaching is concentrated in this chapter.

Broad functions of visual materials used for listening activities

1 To motivate the student to want to find out more by listening.

2 To make him feel that what he is listening to relates to real people, and a real way of life.

3 To provide him with a clue to the meaning of detail.

4 To provide him with a clue to the meaning of gist.

5 To provide him with material by which he can indicate non-verbally that he has understood.

6 To provide him with a graphic analysis of the sound features of the spoken language, for example, by diagrams of intonation patterns.

1 Teaching the meaning of new items

How can the teacher help the learner to understand the meaning behind items in the foreign language? And what about visuals?

Translation, direct method, contextualisation and grammatical description are some of the methods used in the teaching of language. Visual materials can be used in all of these methods at some time.

Translation

Translation into the mother tongue can often convey something of the meaning of many foreign language words or grammatical structures to a level satisfactory to both teacher and pupils.

However, there are also many occasions when no mother tongue equivalent or explanation can quite translate the full degree of meaning the teacher would like to convey to the pupils.

Below are three categories of words and meanings in which visual materials may contribute to the pupils' understanding.

Cultural differences — physical objects and social behaviour

Physical objects   A translation can convey the function of the English word 'letterbox', but cannot fully convey what an English letterbox looks like. A colour picture of a British letterbox would thus add to the student's understanding and would supply all the information he would need to recognise one in the street in Britain.

Social behaviour   Ways of greeting, behaving at table, or of conveying anger or deference vary from country to country and of course within a country. These physical ways of behaving are important for successful communication and are not taught easily by description in the mother tongue. The general concept of the expression 'table manners' can be satisfactorily translated into many languages but what is actually meant by various English speakers can most satisfactorily be conveyed by means of film or television.

Cultural differences — abstract concepts   Frequently, although there is an apparent equivalent in the mother tongue for a word in the foreign language, the concept itself may be rather different.

Democracy can be defined as government by the people, direct or representative. If that is all it is, then such a concept should be easy to teach to a foreign person in either his mother tongue or in English. But is that all that it means? From that definition would foreign people know what is meant when a native speaker uses the word? Another English speaking person may well have a different interpretation, but at least he will probably start from a similar type of assumption. It is this background and the assumptions to which it has given rise which a teacher may want to introduce to the students.

A documentary film approach would provide a means whereby the appreciation as well as the knowledge of the students could be increased. However, such films, we can assume, are not available to the teacher. He could achieve a great deal by compiling a folder containing photocopies of letters, newspaper articles, official proclamations, parliamentary speeches, speeches from the hustings, lists of candidates and their political allegiance, voting patterns, eligibility definitions, graphs, charts and flow charts showing the electoral procedure. Photographs and cartoons might be used to illustrate the voting system and instances of the right of the individual to make representations to his Member of Parliament, to the government, and to stand on a soap box in Hyde Park and attack the lot of them!

These illustrations only tackle some of the meanings associated with democracy. It may well be that the reader would have chosen other aspects.

For many teachers and their students the very general definition above might be satisfactory; the probability of inaccurate assumptions based on their own experience may not be important. If it *is* important that the students get a feeling of what is meant by democracy to an Englishman, then a variety of visual materials may make a considerable contribution to the facts and attitudes which lie behind the word.

Presumably, the teacher and students would use such a massive coverage for more than just the teaching of the associated meanings of the word democracy.

Direct Method

Pictures have always been associated with the Direct Method of teaching foreign languages. It is pointed out that a picture of an object is usually easier to bring into the classroom than the object itself, for example, a bus or an elephant. Also a picture can often show an action more easily than even a talented actor can demonstrate, for example, 'going for a ride' or 'parachuting'!

Contextualisation

Another way of teaching the meaning of language new to the learner is to put it into a context. The context may be solely a language context, for example, a sentence or a short story. Often language already known to the student is combined with pictures and sound effects on tape to tell a story. If the student understands the story, it is hoped he will understand the meaning of the new language.

This method of teaching meaning is common to many of the audio-visual courses of recent years. Usually the language is reproduced on tape or record and the accompanying sequence of pictures on filmstrip or in the pupils' book.

Stories and dialogues are not the only way in which 'new' language can be contextualised. Consider the following examples.

A map of a town can help the teacher to contextualise the language needed for giving and understanding directions.

This sequence of simple blackboard drawings made by the teacher helps to contextualise 'running back home'. The drawing which actually illustrates 'running back home' could, of course, be interpreted as 'running to the house' or just running. However, the sequence as a whole indicates that he is running back home.

Fig. 1

Pictures are not the only type of visual material which can be used to teach meaning.

The demonstration of a simple scientific experiment or of a magic trick makes use of visual materials in a dynamic way. One magic trick fairly easy to describe in the short space here is the following:

The teacher, unknown to the class, puts a small coin between the back of his fingers and then, with outstretched and apparently empty hands, he says 'Oh dear, I haven't got any money'. 'Any money' and 'some money' are the new teaching points. 'Oh dear, what shall I do?' he adds, or other similar patter. Then he rubs his hands together and, while bemoaning his poverty, transfers the coin to the palm of one hand. Then he says, 'Oh. What's this! I've got some money! I've got a penny!'

The teacher repeats this until the children have seen the trick. One pupil is then asked to come to the front and try out the trick and the language himself.

Grammatical description of the foreign language

The meanings conveyed by the grammatical characteristics of the foreign language are usually explained and discussed in the mother tongue. It is often not appreciated that visual materials have a role to play in helping the student to understand these meanings. Examples are given and discussed in the chapter on Grammar, pages 48 to 51.

The choice of contexts and the teaching of meaning

In this section I have listed a few suggestions which might help the teacher and materials producer to find an efficient way of teaching meaning.

1 The new language is most likely to be understood if it is absolutely essential to the context in which it is introduced. This is an important point, often ignored. Another point, also often ignored in practice, though accepted in principle, is to make the context and what the student actually does of interest to him.

In discussing horoscopes and in predicting the future, one is very much thinking about what will happen. Language used for talking about the future could, therefore, be well introduced in such a theme. 'Next week you will be very happy, although

Fig. 2

your work will be difficult and a friend will let you down . . . .'
Visual materials may consist of a horoscope from a newspaper
or magazine. Diaries and calendars can also be used very effectively to make the students think of the future whilst using language
which refers to the future.

Lottery tickets or a newspaper photograph of a winner of the
football pools would help to lead the student's mind to — 'If I
won a lot of money, I would . . . .' (Fig. 2).

2 The students' thinking is also directed towards a specific meaning
if a situation is chosen in which the new language can be contrasted with its opposite. If we want to teach 'thin' it is helpful
to teach 'fat' at the same time, or 'can' and 'can't' at the same
time. The qualities are emphasised through contrast. (Fig. 38)
(See also Chapter on Grammar.)

3 Sometimes it is better to contrast the idea you are teaching with
something similar but nevertheless distinct. In Fig. 94 the fifth
drawing could well be interpreted as 'running' until the fourth
drawing is made. The sense of sprinting in the fifth drawing
becomes apparent when the actions are compared. (See also
Chapter on Grammar.)

4 Another way of directing the students' thinking is to show several
or even many examples of pictures illustrating the new teaching
point. This method may be essential when the meaning of the
new item is not apparent in a single example or when it is impossible to give an opposite which would make the meaning clear.
(Fig. 39).

5 Sometimes we can only understand what is referred to by knowing
what has led up to it. For example the pattern containing 'after'
followed by the present participle might be taught by the
following example:

Fig. 3
He was sick
after eating mushrooms.

Sometimes it is not possible to have more than one picture to illustrate
a concept which is very much part of or the result of a previous event.
Fig. 4 is a flash card used to aid the students' practice of 'se reposer'
(to rest). The account below shows the difficulties involved in illustrating

. Fig. 4

'to rest' in a single picture. The first trial sketches I drew for this subject showed a man leaning on a rake, a man sitting next to a machine and a man sitting in a deckchair. I showed these three sketches to ten people, saying: 'What is he doing?' For the first picture the majority of replies were: 'He's gardening', for the second: 'He's having his break', and for the third, 'He's relaxing', or 'He's sitting in a deckchair'.

I knew, therefore, that it was necessary to find a subject where it was implied that there had been exertion but which was not too easy to name. Also, there should be the implication that there was further action to come. And lastly, that there was no other apparent reason for the person's sitting down than for a rest.

The flash card actually illustrated here contains these elements. To the question 'What is she doing?' the choice is likely to fall between 'She is resting' or 'Having a rest' and 'She is sitting' is improbable because the mass of shopping, her resting posture and the absence of any other reason for being there point to something more specific. Note, if houses had been drawn in the background, it might have elicited 'She is going home'; if a park, including people and perhaps ducks, had been

Fig. 5

shown, this might have elicited 'She is sitting down', i.e. to enjoy the park. Of the ten people asked, nine said, 'She is resting'.

Although asking ten people for their interpretation in this way is hardly a scientifically controlled or widely sampled experiment, it is of use. In hearing the views of a number of people one becomes more conscious of the variety of interpretations which may be given for any one picture. One also becomes conscious of the many different aspects of pictures which are 'read' by the people who see them. For the teacher a quick sampling of the course materials by a few students will give him a considerable insight into the difficulties they may have in interpreting the pictures in the intended way.

(Other aspects of the use of visual materials and the teaching of meaning are also discussed in the chapters on Grammar and Perception.)

Further reading 25, 32, 38, 39

2 Listening discrimination

In this activity the student learns to discriminate between the sounds of the foreign language, many of which will be quite unfamiliar to him. He must concentrate on listening to very slight changes of sound. When visuals are used they are normally pared down to give the minimum amount of information, the aim being to prevent unnecessary distraction.

Example 1 Signs, symbols and diagrams can give a variety of help in listening discrimination work. Materials include charts of phonetic signs and diagrams of intonation and stress patterns in books or on transparencies. (Fig. 11)

Example 2 The meaning implied by stress patterns may be made clearer with pictures.

Fig. 6

(a) Is that *your* dog?
(b) Is *that* your dog?

The pictures may be used to present the meaning of the stress for the first time to the student. Alternatively, he may show his understanding of the different stress patterns by indicating the appropriate picture. Visual character: This is a teacher—made visual. The pinmen convey enough information for the pupil to show whether or not he has discriminated correctly. There is no need, as fas as this activity is concerned, for any further information.

Example 3   To concentrate the pupil's attention on individual sounds a pupil or a group might sort out a large number of separate pictures according to initial sounds.

Example 4   To concentrate the pupil's attention on individual words within a sentence the teacher could make true or false statements about a picture. A statement is made false by a minor sound change. The pupils show whether or not they have discriminated correctly either by showing a 'Yes' or 'No' card or by saying, 'It's true' or 'It's not true'.

Fig. 7   Teacher: **This is a ship.**
Pupil: **It's not true.**

Visual character: Enough information to make it clearly a sheep. Use a flash card rather than a wallchart or book for speed and for concentration on the one item.

3   Extensive and intensive listening

Definition as used in this book:

Extensive listening   The student attempts to understand the gist of what he hears.

Intensive listening   The student attempts to understand a high proportion of what he hears or a high proportion of a certain part of the text.

Texts intended for extensive or intensive listening are frequently accompanied by sequences of pictures or single pictures, helping the student to see the context of what he is hearing and often helping him to understand certain parts of the text.

Visual materials can also be used to aid in the general development of listening skills and to test whether the student has grasped the meaning of the text. The theme of the text and pictures need not be stark and dreary as so many test pictures are. Theme and pictures can recreate in the classroom the situations in which one needs to listen intensively, for example, to the weather forecast on the radio or to a railway announcer. Alternatively, amusing game-like activities can be used.

The examples below are of the 'practice and test' variety. It is clear from these examples that the media and choice of visual style are made according to the character of the theme rather than to any rule about the use of visuals in listening practice.

Extensive listening

Example 1 The student listens to a story on the tape. He attempts to fathom out what is going on. When the story is finished he, or his group, is given a pile of separate pictures which must be put in the correct sequence according to the story.

Alternatively, the pictures, printed or drawn by the teacher in an incorrect order, could be in the pupil's book, on a wallchart or projected. Each picture would be given a number. The pupil would then indicate the correct sequence with these numbers.

Example 2 A dialogue is played to the students. Then a composite picture including a great number of people talking in groups is shown. The students are asked to identify which two people they heard talking and why.

Visual character: The information in the picture must be presented clearly. An impressionistic or expressive style would be distracting and would tend to hide the detail which the students must notice in the picture. Difficulty can be added by providing false clues, by deliberately illustrating some references in the dialogue in several places in the picture. This latter 'difficulty' might be considered useful in that it deliberately increases the choice open to the student.

Intensive listening

Example 1 Each pupil is given a map of Britain and a set of weather symbols. He listens to the weather forecast played to him and records on the map, by means of symbols, the weather for the next day. Alternatively, he is told that he is on holiday with his friends in a certain region and must only listen out for the forecast for that region.

Example 2
The picture on the left is shown to the pupils

Fig. 8

The last words of a dying man have been recorded, also the account of someone who caught sight of a man acting suspiciously. The pupil must listen to both accounts, pick out reference to personal details and indicate the murderer. Note, some of the features will be common to several of the suspected men.

Example 3   A number of pictures illustrating specific ideas are displayed to the pupil either in a book, on a chart or on the overhead projector. Each picture is numbered. The teacher reads out sentences appropriate to each of the pictures. The pupils either write down the relevant numbers or indicate the relevant picture.

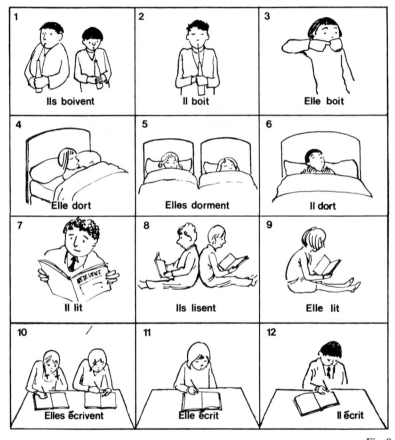

Fig. 9

Example 4   The student is given a map of a town showing buildings as well as street names. He studies it. Then a tape is played to him which purports to be of someone visiting the town for the first time and making a telephone call to explain to his host that he is quite lost. The little street where his host lives is not shown on the map. The host first establishes where his visitor is, then gives him instructions about which way to go to find his home.

The student must also establish where on the map the visitor is and then track down and locate the street where he must go to.

Visual character: It could be presented like a tourist map issued by the tourist information office.

Example 5 Maps are very useful for listening work. Here is another example, this time concentrating particularly on prepositions of place. The teacher draws a very simple street map showing rectangles for buildings, some of which are named.

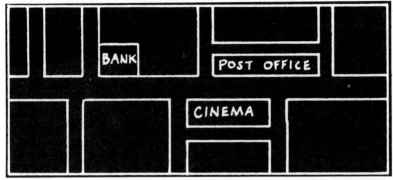

Fig. 10

One method of exploiting this drawing is by team competition. The class is divided into two teams, each team sending a player to the board.

One player describes orally the position of a place on the map. For example,

'There is a butcher's shop opposite the bank.' (The bank is drawn on the plan.) The other pupil must draw the butcher's shop in the appropriate position and label it. Points are given. Alternatively, this activity may be done in pairs.

Example 6 Eight photographs of famous people are reproduced or cut from magazines. A tape is played which contains the descriptions of their lives. The pupils must indicate which description relates to which person.

Example 7 Bingo. The pupils each have a card which they divide into nine squares. In each of these squares they write a number (or word of whatever language it is the teacher would like to concentrate on). The teacher then calls out numbers (or words referring to the objects or actions depicted). Pupils with those numbers cover them up or cross them out. The first one with a card completed wins.

Example 8 A sequence of pictures is shown to the students and a taped story is played. The story contains a number of details inconsistent with the pictures. The students are asked to look at the pictures, then listen to the story, noting any inconsistencies they hear.

2 Speaking

The neat categories used in this chapter should not be seen as exclusive. Other skills will be integrated with these activities, and these activities may be seen as a part of role playing and the training for 'survival' in particular situations: for example, travelling in the foreign country, dealing with an accident. Some examples given below have actually been extracted from integrated materials with such 'survival situations' in mind.

Themes are another way of integrating the various activities described below. A general theme of interest to the students is presented and worked on through textual and visual material. Structures and vocabulary are learnt in order to understand more of the theme and to be better able to express one's opinions about it. Several examples in the chapter are given from such theme work.

Broad functions of visual materials used for speaking activities

1 To motivate the student to want to speak.

2 To create a context within which his speech will have meaning.

3 To provide the student with information to use in speech, including objects, actions, events, relationships.

4 To provide the student with non-verbal cues for manipulation work.

5 To provide non-verbal prompts to dialogue reproduction or to dialogue invention.

I Repetition

The student's total concentration must be on listening to the spoken model and then on the imitation of it. If visual materials are to be used there should be a minimum of distracting information in the picture. Of course, the teacher may be happy to risk a little distraction if there is a gain in other ways: for example, through a humorous quality in the picture or by a flavour of the foreign culture.

There is often a time when the teacher would like the pupil to concentrate on distinguishing finely differentiated sounds and on trying to produce those sounds himself. He may present these sounds as isolated phonemes or in words, phrases or sentences. There is a wealth of published visual material available to help with this type of work. There are diagrams showing mouth, tongue and teeth positions; signs showing intonation and stress when speaking from a written text. There are gadgets, games, charts and flash cards which show text pictures or one of these without the other. (See also Oral Reading page 32).

Even though the emphasis is on training the student to distinguish new sounds and to produce them, there is no reason why the meaning of the words should be ignored. There are a number of simple ways of achieving this.

Example 1   The teacher makes a number of statements about a picture. The pupils only repeat those which are reasonable. Alternatively, an element of interest and also a reason for hearing individuals speak can be given by a number of games. One very simple game is to have two packs of pictures: the teacher keeps one pack and the other identical pack is distributed one, two or three cards to each child. The teacher says, 'It's a dog'. The pupils listen intensively and directed by their cards, repeat after the teacher if *they* have that card.

Example 2   The following symbols are listed by Mackey to represent stress and intonation. (Further reading 60).

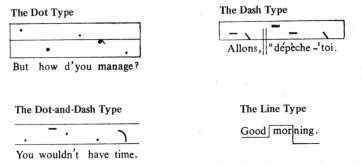

The Dot Type

But   how   d'you   manage?

The Dash Type

Allons,   "dépèche -'toi.

The Dot-and-Dash Type

You wouldn't   have time.

The Line Type

Good ⌐mor⌐ning.

Fig. 11   **Rhythm and intonation**

Example 3   Dialogues are often used for repetition work. A sequence of pictures accompanying the dialogue introduces the meaning, and gives it a believable setting (for example, Fig. 74). The role of the pictures in creating a sense of a real place and a real event is valuable particularly in the early years of language learning. The ideas which can be dealt with in the language known to the student are often below his sophistication. Pictures can compensate for this.

The pictures may also act as a reminder of meaning as the student struggles to remember long stretches of text.

There is in the points above the idea that the pictures help to make the meaning clear and memorable and also that they add a feeling of reality of place. Thus a balance should be struck between the need to avoid distracting information and the amount of information necessary to make it look 'real'.

Example 4   The pupil repeats after the teacher or the taped voice. The pictures contextualise what the pupil is saying.

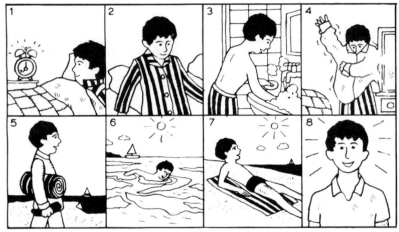

Repeat: 1. Voici Pierre. Il s'est réveillé à sept heures.
         2.   Il s'est levé.
         3.   Il s'est lavé dans la salle de bains.
         etc.   Fig. 12

2 Reproduction

The main role of visual material used to aid reproduction activities is to act as a reminder, by association, of what the students have previously learnt, and as a specific cue to the language now required. The visual may also add fun, relate the activity to a real-life situation or turn the activity into an event in its own right.

Picture flash cards, composite pictures, sequences of pictures and figurines may all be used in this way. The most usual method is for the teacher to ask a question and to proffer the picture or other visual material as a cue to the answer. Obviously, visual material used for repetition is often useable for reproduction. Example 4 having been used for repetition may be used for reproduction, by giving the question: 'A quelle heure est-ce qu'il s'est réveillé?' The answer will be the relevant phrase previously repeated and learnt.

The characteristics of visual material used for reproduction activities will normally be the same as those used for repetition, i.e. simplicity and immediacy of reference to the language involved.

Example 1 This is one of the many ways of showing a picture sequence to the pupil to guide him and remind him of what to say. In this case the pictures are printed on a card which the pupil can hold while he narrates a story or takes part in a dialogue.

Visual character: The drawings are bare of all unnecessary information, the drawing style is unobtrusive, the layout is clear. Pinmen drawings (see page 118) would be very serviceable. Photographs, stylised drawings, complex drawings would have distracting qualities.

Fig. 13

Example 2 There are various 'nice ideas' which may appeal to certain age groups. One of these is to teach conjuring tricks which have a certain

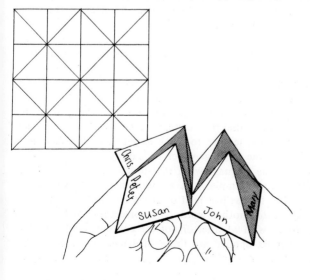

Fig. 14

pattern of commentary. You perform the trick for the pupils, then invite them to practise it so they can perform it at home for their parents – in the foreign language. In this way a considerable amount of repetition is done associated with action and, of course, fun.

Here is an example:

Teacher: 'I am going to put this piece of chalk under this piece of paper. Now, I am going to pick up the piece of chalk but I am not going to pick up the piece of paper!

KABOOM!! Come here, please!' (beckons pupil). 'Pick up the piece of paper.' (pupil does so) Teacher picks up the chalk and says: 'I picked up the piece of chalk but I didn't pick up the piece of paper!'

A device which may be of fun to the under 12's and to the over 20's is the paper fortune teller common in British school playgrounds and described in Opie p 342 (Opie, I. and P. *Lore and Language of School-children,* OUP, 1959). Various standard types of question can be worked out for this fortune telling and reproduced as the pupil works the paper gadget for his friends.

3   Manipulation

The student may make changes in the sentence pattern, for example, using a different part of the paradigm, or he may substitute various vocabulary items. Whatever sort of manipulative work is going on the learner will usually concentrate on relatively isolated concepts. The teacher, however, may want to deliberately complicate the context in which the student is manipulating the language in order to simulate more closely conditions in the foreign country and perhaps to test the student, to see if he has a confident grasp of the problem. The character of the visual material will reflect these intentions.

One thing which is particularly important in manipulative work is the need to *vary* the contexts in which the student uses the teaching item. He should become familiar with it in a variety of settings. This variety may be obtained by a number of separate pictures showing instances or with a composite picture containing a number of instances.

Increasingly in manipulative work and even more in composition, the material should involve the learner intellectually and emotionally. Materials and methods can cause the learner to think as much of the idea he is trying to communicate as the language which he is using.

As often as possible the language work the student does should not be arbitrary in meaning: for example, it is a common practice to ask the student to change what he has just read or heard to another part of the paradigm or to substitute another word. The correctness of his answer has often nothing to do with whether or not the content of what he says matters. The sole criteria applied are those of agreements etc. Practice in the mechanical manipulation of language may contribute something but so too will manipulation of the language to express the wishes, opinions, ideas and purposes of the speaker.

The emphasis the teacher puts on fun, real life reference, or stark functionalism will determine the sort of visual to be used. A real questionnaire or graph or timetable might be used or a mechanical device for controlling sentence patterns (Fig. 17). Styles of drawing may vary from naturalistic to cartoon.

Example 1   Oral exercises in which the stress is on the correct mechanical manipulation of language can be given support by visual materials. A very common use of the visual in the pupil's book or the flash card, for example, is to offer, by picture, a cue to an alternative part of a sentence.

For example, any of the pictures below may be used to cue an alternative object in the sentence, to complete a sentence, or to provide an answer to a question. If the pictures are drawn on cards the teacher may hold one of them up or point if they are drawn on a wallchart.

Fig. 15

Yesterday I went into town and bought some apples.

Yesterday I went into town and bought a hat.

What did you do yesterday?

I bought some shoes.

Other simple pictures may be used as cues for various means of transport, for various destinations, actions, etc.

Example 2 The picture diagrams intended to cue manipulative work in the *Longman Audio-Visual French Course* (Longman, 1968) are very well designed. They are very simple and usually clear. The design element directs the activity by means of arrowed boxes.

Fig. 16
Exemple
La vieille dame. . .
Elle a laissé son sac
dans le train

1
2
3
4
5

1 Yves . . .
2 M. Patou . . .
3 M. Patou . . .
4 La vielle dame . . .
5 Le gros monsieur . . .

Example 3 Column diagrams are used very frequently for substitution exercises. Such diagrams printed in the pupil's book or on workcards or on large class charts are usually perfectly adequate. However, the fact that all the alternatives can be seen at any one time may not be what the teacher wants. There are several devices for overcoming this. (One of them is illustrated below.)

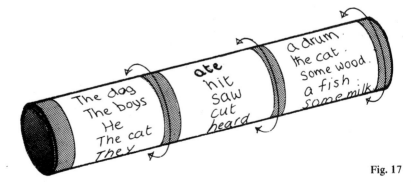

Fig. 17

By rotating the segments separately new combinations of words are made. The device can be so made that in one position all the sentences make up a logical account. Alternatively in some positions many of the sentences make sense, but they all make sense in only one position.

Such devices not only help the concentration on a selection of the alternatives but they have the *physical qualities* which so many, particularly young people, appreciate.

Example 4 In the first three examples given above there is very little concern with the meaning of the language used.

Examples 4-9 show ways in which the learners might be caused to think about the ideas implied by the language.

Example 4 provides a very pleasant but meaningful way of manipulating:
'If I had a lot of money I would . . .'

Fig. 18

Example 5 'The artist has made 20 mistakes in copying the first picture. Can you find them?'

This particular example is helpful in those languages which have a complex system of agreements.

Jeu des vingt erreurs
Sur son deuxième dessin, notre dessinateur a fait vingt erreurs. Pouvez-vous les retrouver?

Fig. 19

Example 6 These two drawings provide a subject for discussion expressing possession.

Fig. 20

Example 7 Horoscopes. The students look up the prediction for their month. They discuss the prediction with their neighbour manipulating the paradigm from 'I' to 'you'. The teacher can then introduce 'he', 'she', 'they' in a number of ways, for example, the teacher might give the Prime Minister's birthday and ask what will happen to him.

Example 8 A sequence of simple drawings which perhaps make a humorous story or depict a crime; no text is given or very little. The pupils study the pictures in silence then put them away. The teacher asks questions using a past tense. 'What happened?' 'What did he do first?' etc.

Fig. 21

Example 9 (Role Playing Cards)   The pupils are divided into pairs. Each pupil has a different card from his partner. On the card is a series of questions to ask the other pupil and a series of *answers* to the questions of the *other* pupil. These answers are printed in the second plural form 'vous'. The pronoun and paradigm ending must be changed appropriately.

Visual character: The fact that the text is printed on card rather than in a book helps the teacher to control what each pupil sees. It gives the feeling to the pupil that the card is his own and he can thus identify better with the role he is expected to play.

Example 10   The composite picture (Fig. 65) may be used to give manipulative practice in, for example, the model sentence 'While I was standing on the street corner, I saw two men pushing a car.' The teacher tells the students to imagine that they are the policeman and to make parallel sentences.

4   Composition

Without visual material it is very difficult for the teacher to create a situation in which the students want to say something. Even with a picture the student is not likely to respond if merely told to 'say something about it'.

The teacher must present pictures and other materials in a way which is relevant to the interests and age of his students. In fact, this material should be of interest to the students whether they are in or out of the language classroom.

The visual character of material used for composition will, if successful, reflect concern for relevance to the students' interests. The material will also provoke individual responses. We are not sure what the student will say: he communicates his ideas to us by means of the target language. To provide for these individual interpretations, there should be a certain complexity in or implied by the material. Ambiguity, a quality not usually desirable in pictures intended to contribute to the understanding of meaning, will be welcome here. In addition, the teacher may want to simulate the foreign setting of the language activity. This too will be reflected in the medium chosen and the visual design of it.

Guided composition

The teacher may want to launch the learner out into composition but feel that he needs a guide line. Visual materials can very usefully supply non-verbal prompts for this purpose. The student must supply all the language, but the material gives him something to talk about and guides him to use the language the teacher knows he can manage.

Visual character: The key phrase above is 'guide line'. If the intention is to guide the student then the material must not present more alternatives than are required.

The factor of cultural reference is not directly related to the activity of guided composition: it involves a separate decision. The quantity of cultural information (road signs, houses, styles of clothes etc.) given in the picture depends on how far the teacher feels it is important to simulate a foreign context for the students' work.

Example 1   This picture sequence is taken from *SCOPE,* the 'English for Immigrants' Project (*Scope, Picture Book 1,* Longman, 1969). The abbreviated teacher's notes read: 'These pictures tell the story of a family leaving Cyprus by boat and arriving in England. Use when talking about pupils' own journeys. Contrast boats with planes making use of Wall Picture 1.'

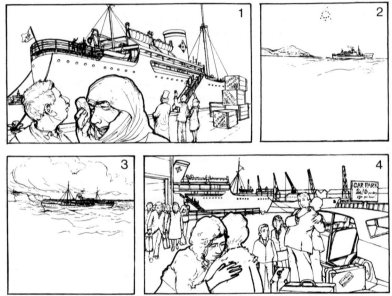

Fig. 22

Visual character: Considerable cultural information is supplied in these pictures, but on the other hand only those events and objects relevant to a central theme are shown. This control of information is, of course, easier to show by line drawing than photograph.

Note: by seeing the four pictures together the pupil has a better chance of understanding the gist of the story than if they were shown separately as on filmstrip. Unfortunately, some students reported that they did not realise that the two ships are supposed to be the same one. Is this because they seem to be going in different directions?

Example 2 One way of doing this is for the teacher to make the first drawing at the extreme left-hand side of the blackboard and to invite any pupil to supply a relevant phrase. Any pupil supplying a relevant commentary may go to the board and add a second drawing. As new drawings are added and the story grows each pupil adding a phrase must also repeat all preceding phrases, using the drawings as cues. This activity involves a large amount of speaking reproduction but also some crucial inventive composition work.

Fig. 23   A sequence of pinmen drawings on the blackboard

Example 3 A single picture, particularly if related to a story previously read or a topic discussed, could be used to guide oral composition. A single picture without such connections with previous language work would probably present a whole range of interpretations more suitable for unguided composition.

Example 4 Non-pictorial material may also be used for the same effect. Graphs, charts and other statistical material might be used to guide a discussion along certain lines.

A very successful idea is to ask the pupil to draw a map explaining how he gets to school. He then uses this map to plan a narrative description of what he sees and does, and uses it again to cue himself while he speaks about it.

Incidentally if the pupil has drawn on a transparency, his map can be projected on the overhead projector and will then act as a guide for the other pupils who are listening and give them something to question him on.

Unguided composition

Whereas the visual materials used in the early stages of the learning sequence are usually most appropriate when unambiguous and unadorned with redundant information, the visual materials for composition may be all the better for these very qualities. In the early stages the teacher is pointing, by means of the visual, to a particular concept; in the later stages he is hoping that the *student* will point to concepts of concern to himself by using the foreign language.

The visual qualities of successful materials used for composition cannot be specified. They may contain a mass of detail or very little, be photographs, cartoons, graphs or questionnaires. What they have in common is the quality of stimulating the student to want to say something of his own.

The teacher's only restriction, apart from practical ones, will be to attempt to avoid provoking ideas which are quite beyond the student's power to express himself in the target language.

Detailed exploitation by the teacher is not described in this book, partly for reasons of space, partly because every teacher's case will be unique. However, one general point which may be worth passing on is this: encourage the students to say something, however little. Unguided composition as described above, does not preclude humble comments like, 'That's a black dog.'

Example 1   What are they saying? The magazine *Private Eye* has made much use of this type of captioning of photographs.

Fig. 24

Example 2 For another sort of speculative picture see *What Do You Think?* (Further Reading 17). Although the less able students might give short descriptive comments or make 'Yes', or 'No' answers to the teacher's questions, the main intention is that only open questions should be put which demand speculation about the picture.

'Why is she looking through the window?'
'What will she do next?'
'Who is she?'

Example 3 In social studies and English studies it is increasingly common to do a lot of work on a theme. This sort of work which, in adapted form, can be used in E.F.L. situations, is briefly described below. Text written and taped, pictures, graphs and questionnaires are built up on a topic or theme. The topic may be of national importance, e.g. unemployment, or of local importance, e.g. 'Should we have a pop festival in our town?'

The material sets the scene, gives the views of the different people involved, both their feelings and the interpretation of factual happenings. Statistical and similarly concrete facts are also given.

This mass of audio-visual information is studied, usually by groups of students. They debate it as outsiders or take on the roles of the people described.

If interest is sustained the teacher could ask each group to finalise, by discussion, one new point and then to debate that viewpoint with the class as a whole.

This might provide just the sort of stimulating and relevant work necessary for advanced students of the foreign language. For those students less well advanced, more hidden structuring by the teacher would have to take place.

Example 4 One way of keeping the subject within the bounds of the learner's speaking abilities in the foreign language is to provide useful and relevant written language for them. It is particularly useful if this is presented on separate cards. The teacher can control what each person sees and when he sees it. The card is also easier to hold if there is any debating or role playing to do.

Example 5 Pictures taken from various sources and juxtaposed can stimulate strong personal reactions. These pictures are easily collected from the mass of printed material which floods our homes. The examples on pages 28-29 are taken from *What Do You Think?* Book 2.

What are these pets? Whose are they? Which do you like? Have you got a pet? Is this pet common in your country? Which is the most common pet in your country? (Teacher and pupils carry out a questionnaire-survey.) Why do you think that person has that pet? What is their relationship? Do you think it right to keep pets when half the world is starving?

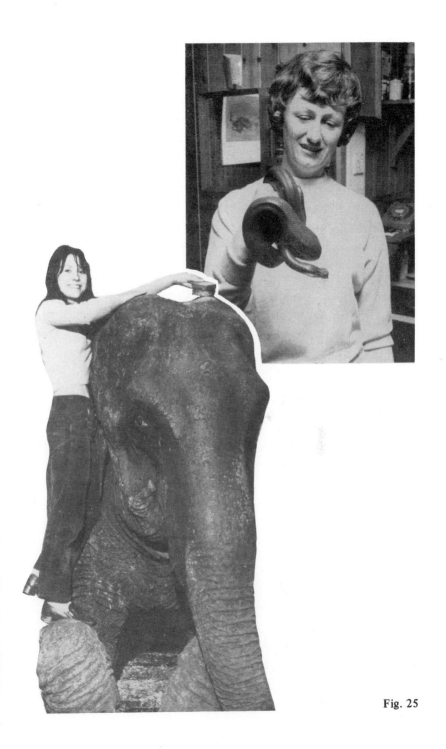

Fig. 25

Example 6   Everybody's dream of receiving a lot of money can be stimulated by the type of picture in Fig. 2 and described and discussed in the class. 'Would you give it to the poor? Would you buy a beautiful painting? What would *you* do with the money?'

On the other hand, the picture could be described and the students could speculate about how they think the farmer and his family will spend the money.

Further reading 17, 26, 80

3 Reading

There are three sections in this chapter. Under the first section, Oral reading, are those activities which relate to the association of written symbols with spoken sounds. In these activities the main emphasis is *not* on getting meaning from the text. The next two sections relate closely to the activities described under listening, namely:

Extensive reading: the student attempts to understand the gist of what he reads.

Intensive reading: the student attempts to understand a high proportion of what he reads.

Broad functions of visual materials used for writing activities

1 To motivate the student to want to read.

2 To make him feel that what he is reading and the way he is reading it relate to the way in which written text is used in real life.

3 To provide a clue to the meaning of detail, either introducing him to the meaning for the first time or reminding him of it.

4 To provide a clue to the gist of the passage or text, either introducing it to him for the first time or reminding him of a theme previously met.

5 To provide extra information over and above that given in the text, perhaps to make the general experience more interesting by compensating for the limitations of the language.

6 To provide him with material by which he may indicate non-verbally that he has understood.

7 To provide him with a symbolic analysis of the relation between written language and spoken sounds.

Visual character of materials for reading

Visual material can be used to contribute to the functions listed above. The form and the design of the material will be dependent on the function chosen. Thus no more specific a generalisation can be made than that.

For example, if the sole function is to give meaning to a specific part of the text, then there should be no information irrelevant to that function in the visual. On the other hand the visual may be used to heighten the drama of the storyline as conveyed in the text, in which case a totally different mode of visual presentation might be used.

I Oral reading

Visual materials are used to aid the recognition of letter forms, groups of letters, single words and groups of words and their relation to sounds. Phonic work and more generally oral reading (reading aloud) is usually introduced when oral fluency is established. At this stage, the pupil will be unable, and should not be expected, to read and pronounce accurately words with which he is not familiar.

Example 1   One of the most successful aspects of the primary materials of the *French Pilot Course* (Nuffield Foundation Foreign Language Materials Project) was the introduction to reading. The role of the visual was vital to this stage of the French materials. The transition from speaking to reading was achieved in the following way:

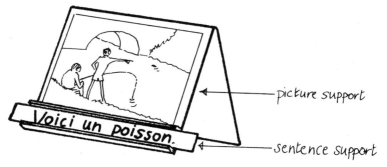

Fig. 26

1 Short dialogues illustrated with sequences of eight still pictures were learnt and practised orally.
2 After the sentences, and their relation to certain pictures, were well known orally, the same sentences, printed individually on strips of card, were put beneath the appropriate picture. The pupil then read the sentence. It should be remembered that this is only a transitional stage between speaking and reading.
3 The third stage in the sequence was to give to the pupils a reader in which the same pictures were illustrated with some of the same sentences. Some new sentences were also introduced to take the pupil one step nearer to being able to recognise the relationship of written symbol and spoken sound without an immediate model.

Example 2 The first example takes the pupil immediately to the recognition of complete sentences. There are many ways of relating single written words or parts of words to sounds. A very common way is by picture and sound matching. A jumbled pile of pictures and a jumbled pile of words relating to those pictures is sorted out into sound groups. The pupil may first put all pictures together with the same initial sounds and then sort out the written words and put the appropriate one with each picture.

Example 3 There are a number of ways of giving the pupil the written text, the spoken version of it and pictorial material to cue meaning.

Media and materials include large wall sheets, flash cards, overhead projector transparencies, sentence makers, cards and readers displaying text and accompanied by a taped voice or the teacher's voice reading the text. (See Chapter on Media).

Example 4 Oral reading with the main emphasis on the correct recognition of the relationship between sound and written symbol need not preclude the student's being aware of meaning. The example here is modest but, nevertheless, makes the student think of the meaning of the words he is reading.

Pupil 1: Chooses a flash card from a pile, each card showing one sentence, e.g.
    'Why are you putting your jacket on?'
He reads it out.

Pupil 2: Chooses a card from another pile, each card giving an answer to a specific statement in the first pile.
    'Because I'm cold.'
He reads it out.

2 Intensive reading

Example 1 (For group work) There are many ways of using flash cards and 'game' cards for reading activities. One of them is described below.

Make 48 cards about 6 cm x 10 cm. Think of 24 sentences, with part of each sentence on 24 of the cards and the remaining part of the sentence on the other 24 cards. On the reverse side of the first 24 write the number '1' and on the reverse side of the second 24 write '2'.

Deal the first pack out to a group of pupils. Put the second pack face down in the middle. The players, in turn, take a card from the central pack. If they can make a sentence they lay it down and it is checked by the others. If it is not accepted, the player replaces a card and misses a turn. The first one to have no cards in his hands is the winner. This

Fig. 27

activity is directed in the sense that the pupils are on the lookout for cards to complete the sentences.

Example 2 A straightforward way of causing directed intensive reading to occur is for the teacher to give the student a card with a number of questions on it, or problems to solve, or unfinished statements to complete; then to direct the student to written texts, perhaps in magazines or wall-charts. The student will scan the text, looking only for the solution to his particular task: for example, given a number of short articles on the daily lives of celebrities — What is their favourite food? Where do each of them like to go on holiday? What do they think of the British?

Advertising posters for events or goods for sale can be used in the same way.

Visual character: Wallcharts and wall displays are one way of presenting the text to be searched. Other ways include single folded cards with the text on one side and the questions facing. Of course the text book is the most common way of presenting the material to be studied. The advantage of not using the text book is the effect of a new mode of presentation, the effect which might simulate real life more closely, i.e. use of magazines or the public display of notices; the possibility of controlling which questions each student answers by printing different sets of questions on different cards.

Example 3 Drawings and text are often used together for instruction in Safety. In the example opposite the drawings help to give meaning to the text, to add information not given in the text and to give a sense of reality to the situation.

Fig. 28

Instructions to do or to make something which is relevant to the student work well as teaching material. The student is interested in the content and realises that the foreign language is a possible source of information rather than being merely a skill to learn.

Visual character: to complement the quality of a 'real life' use of instructions the design, typeface and drawing should if possible be of the kind used normally in published leaflets or on posters. One possibility, if target language material is not available would be to get a first aid poster, to block out the mother tongue text and to print on the instructions in the target language.

Example 4   The pupil could be told that the problems are intended to improve his thinking, i.e. language being used as a means to an end.

An answer could be printed on the reverse side, possibly as part of a multiple choice list. Or the pupil might prepare his own answer, which is then compared with a list of answers kept by the teacher.

It would be quite exciting if there were about 40 of these cards arranged in groups of 10 and printed on different coloured cards. It could be claimed that the whole brain-boosting course was built on four stages of difficulty. In fact the teacher could arrange the cards to coincide with the language difficulties.

Very good ideas may be adapted from *Brain Boosters,* by D. Webster, Pan Books and other encyclopaedias of experiments.

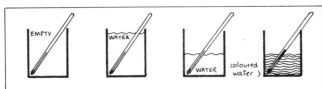

What will happen to the thermometers when these jars are put in the sun? Which will go up the fastest? Which will be the highest after three hours? (Card 1)

The thermometer in the jar without water will go up the fastest when put in the sun. After three hours the thermometer in the coloured water will probably be highest. (Card 2)

Fig. 29

Fig. 30

1. THE GUINNESS PIPELINE.

The pipeline, completed in 1857, runs from the brewery in St. James's Gate, Dublin, passing beneath the Irish Sea and terminating at the Grand Pumping Station in the National Gallery, London. It will long stand as a glorious monument to the eminent Victorian engineer and drinker, Isambard Kingdom O'Brien (1821-1903).

☐ true ☐ false

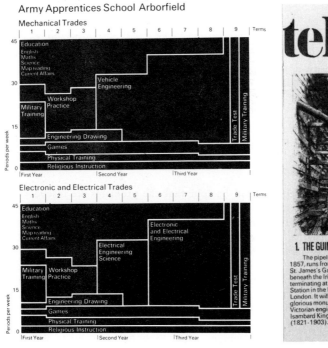

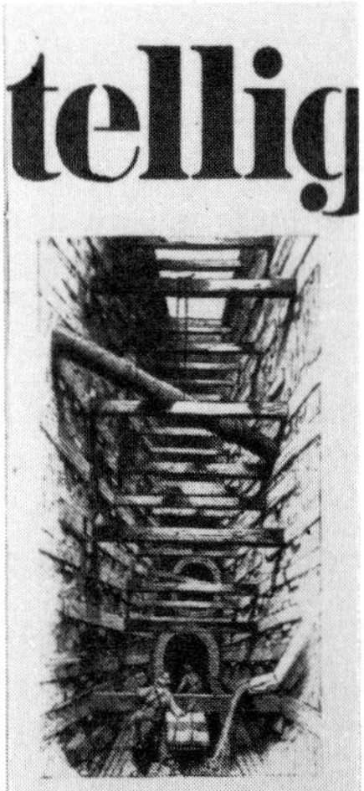

Fig. 31

Example 5   (from Further reading 44)

Questions (see Fig. 30)

1 Give the length of the courses in years, the number of terms per year and the number of periods worked each week. (Each period is forty minutes long.)
2 Name three activities which continue throughout both courses.
3 Compare the two courses and then write down any significant differences you are able to find.
       (Three questions from the ten given by Heath.)
Graphs can be used to give information necessary for answers to be made. The questions above must be read intensively. Heath's book, from which this example is taken, is for mother tongue learners.

3 Extensive reading

Example 1   The picture and text in Fig. 31 were taken from an advertisement entitled, 'Guintelligence'. They are the first of six on a double spread. It is very entertaining to read and excellent in itself for language teaching. either in its present form or in an adapted version. The teacher could easily imitate this idea by taking a number of photographs from magazines and by making true or false statements about them.

Example 2   In this example the visual contributes to the following:
1 motivation,
2 prevention of a totally wrong grasp of the gist of the text,
3 the meaning of certain parts of the text,
4 a clear demonstration of the difference between written language and spoken language, albeit written.

Es ist Freitag morgen. Klasse 4b hat Geographie. Plötzlich sieht Max: es schneit.

Es schneit immer noch. Fabelhaft! sagen Max, Gert und Karl.

Fig. 32

Visual character: The style chosen should be that acceptable to the age group of the learner. Note that comic strip is not exclusively acceptable to adolescents, see *Punch, Private Eye* etc.

Further reading 59

4 Writing

The idea of making the pupil think about language as communication while doing simple repetitive or reproductive work is as applicable here as in speaking. But there will sometimes be justification for a near mechanical use of writing. A few examples are given below to show how even this mechanical work can be given a 'special flavour' with the aid of visual materials.

Broad functions of visual materials used for writing activities

1 To motivate the student.

2 To create a context within which his written text will have meaning.

3 To provide the student with information to refer to, including objects, actions, events, relationships.

4 To provide non-verbal cues for manipulation practice.

5 To provide non-verbal prompts to written composition.

The chapter is divided into five sections: spelling, repetition, reproduction, manipulation and composition. (For a definition of these activities compare Speaking page 14.)

Writing activities will often occur in conjunction with other activities. The examples in this chapter have writing as a main function.

I Spelling

The overhead projector, the magnet board, the word maker and other gadgets all help the teacher to demonstrate the effect of adding, removing and substituting letters.

For the pupil himself it might be an advantage not to have the problem of forming letters when concentrating on spelling. Letters or groups of letters can be given to the pupil on cards which he can then form into words. There are many games for all levels of sophistication designed to test and to improve spelling.

Example 1 A very simple game for two players consists of making a word and then of changing it by the substitution of one letter (and/or the addition of or removal of one letter). The player to make the last change wins the game.

Son, sun, bun, bud, bus . . .

One person could play the game, simply recording how many words he made.

Example 2   Each child has a number of small cards, on each card he writes a letter or group of letters, as instructed by the teacher. The teacher then reads out three or four words beginning with the same letter or the same sound. The pupils select the appropriate card and hold it up.

Example 3   A number of cards are prepared, on one side of which is a picture and on the other the initial letter(s) of the relevant word. These cards are used by pupils working in pairs. The cards are placed vertically in a stand (see page 83 sentence maker). The pupil who can see the picture side of the card says, for example, 'show me a house'. The other pupil points, if he is correct, at the card with the letter 'h' which is facing him. They continue until all the cards have been described and correctly indicated.

Example 4   The students go through a picture magazine and list all the objects or actions which begin with a certain letter or sound. This activity might be done in pairs or groups and done competitively with other groups.

2 Repetition

How can we make the art of copying into an interesting activity? One way might be to copy something in order to possess it and this we do in real life. We copy menus, songs, instructions, directions etc. in our daily life. Another way is to make the activity part of a game.

Example 1   Show a number of cartoons with their captions in a jumbled order. The student must read intensively in order to see where each caption should go and must copy the sentence down perhaps against a number relating to a cartoon or, better still, write it under the cartoon itself.

Visual character: Note that in speaking repetition the model to be copied is transitory; the student must concentrate. In writing repetition the need for single intense concentration is absent − the written model won't go away. Therefore, it is more feasible to add information to the visual material to increase motivation, sense of reality, cultural information etc. without the same fear of the dire results of distraction.

Example 2   Each pupil makes a booklet. Then songs, poems, sayings, menus, instructions for making things are copied into the booklet. These may be mixed or follow a single theme.

Example 3   The pupils write up dialogues on cards which they can hold easily when acting. This is a patently useful reason for copying and one which might well be done in a mother tongue situation.

Example 4   Pupils in groups copy single sentences or words from their books or from the blackboard onto small pieces of card. A group of children can soon, in this way, be equipped with a set of cards for a reading game.

Example 5   The teacher shows the class ten to twelve sentences. Some of these sentences contain reasonable and some false statements. The students read the sentences and copy out the sentences in two lists. Alternatively the students might precede each statement with, 'It is true that . . . .' or 'It is not true that . . . .'.

Example 6   The teacher shows a list of questions and a list of answers in jumbled sequence. The students write down each question and the appropriate answer.

3 Reproduction

Visual material for reproduction activities serves to remind the pupil of the sentence(s) to be reproduced. It provides a link for him with a situation in which he has repeated the sentence or in some way become familiar with it. The material may be interesting, amusing, or have some cultural information, but in principle these features should be subservient to clarity and immediacy of the 'reminding' function.

Various examples are discussed under Speaking reproduction and similar materials under Speaking and Writing repetition.

Example 1   A rather individual type of visual material is the crossword puzzle. Crossword puzzles can be designed to cause various writing activities.

An example is given below, taken from Michael Buckby's article in *AVLA (AVLA* Vol. 8 No. 3 Winter 1970-71).

'To practise the written forms of the Imperfect Tense at the reproduction stage. The class is given a crossword puzzle, the clues of which consist of known sentences with gaps, i.e. the missing words complete the puzzle.

In 1862 bicycles . . . . very big wheels.'

(The clues relate to reading material concerning inventions already encountered by the pupils.)

Example 2   The teacher or the students draw a number of simple pin-men drawings on the board, agree on a suitable caption and write it underneath. When the drawings and sentences are complete the students copy the pinmen drawings. The teacher then removes the sentences and the students endeavour to remember them and to write them next to their drawings. The drawings act as a reminder.

Example 3 The teacher holds up a number of flash cards of words or puts them on the flannelboard, overhead projector or blackboard. The pupils read these silently and endeavour to compose a sentence with them. When the words are removed the sentences are written down.

Example 4- The class is divided into teams. The first player in each team is given a sheet of sentences. After one minute he gives the sheet to the next person in the team, goes to the board and writes down the first sentence. After another minute the second person passes on the sheet and goes to the board to write out the second sentence. The first team to complete the sentences on the board correctly is the winner.

4 Manipulation

Visual materials can help by providing a variety of contexts for the teaching item, which is so necessary at the manipulation stage. Also, if required, they can provide convincing representations and simulations of real life situations in which the language is to be manipulated.

The character of the visual material will be determined by what its contribution is to be.

Example 1 There are a number of materials which concentrate the student's attention on language patterns. These are used for speaking and writing manipulation. They include substitution tables, and the various gadgets described under Media.

These are patently learning aids and should be designed solely with efficiency of use in mind, with clear print and clear layout. If the teacher wants the pupil to be unable to make a mistake then he must design the material in such a way that this is unlikely to happen. For example, whereas it is easy to ensure that the pupil keeps to a constant syntactical order, it is less easy to control the morphological agreements. A free choice might lead to, 'He like dogs.' If the teacher wants to guide the pupil to correct agreements then he must do so by visual design, by lines, arrows etc. depending on the device.

Example 2 Advertisements, notices, announcements are studied and alternative versions are written out. These new versions may be serious, perhaps giving notice of a meeting of a language society, or humorous, making ridiculous claims for a product.

Example 3 Topics can be found in which a limited number of patterns constantly recur. If topics are chosen which are of interest to the student, then he can be guided to use these patterns to communicate personal information.

Recipes written in the target language could provide model patterns which are used by the student in writing out other recipes, e.g. 'Stir continuously for five minutes' might become, 'Stir occasionally for ten minutes' et

A description of a town in the foreign country written in the target language could serve as the model for a description of the student's home town in the target language, with perhaps the aim of giving it to the local tourist office for issue to foreign visitors.

Biographical booklets could be made of the student's hero based on a model. It could be illustrated with photographs and drawings.

In all of these examples there is a total emphasis on the idea communicated by the language. Hence the subject should be of interest to the student. The model and the student's own version should be of the kind he might encounter in real life. If the visual character of the model is patently a production for school, then the work associated with it will probably have that flavour for the student and be seen by him as a sugar-coated device to extract work from him. On the other hand, that may be an extreme and pessimistic view. It may well be that an interesting idea will triumph over an unconvincing visual presentation of it.

5 Composition

Guided composition

Whatever other functions the material may have, providing interest, fun, cultural setting and so on, the main function is that of guiding the student to use his store of the foreign language to communicate his ideas and opinions. The principal criterion will be to provide an interesting stimulus for the student, but one which is not likely to provoke a reaction impossible for him to express with his grasp of the foreign language.

The degree of guidance is directly related to the material the student is given: for example, a sequence of related pictures is more likely to guide the student to use certain language than a general stimulus picture. A sequence of pictures drawn in a 'bare' style with minimal information is more likely to give specific guidance than a sequence of pictures in a convention which gives a mass of information, i.e. detailed drawing style or detailed photographs. (See Realism to Symbolism).

Any accompanying text may also partly determine the student's activity. A series of questions to be answered with the information to be found in the pictures could lead to a very close control of the type of answer given. Alternatively, questions could be given which invite a great variety of interpretations and little control of the language the student selects.

A text can be given with the pictures. If there are gaps in it to be filled by the student the control is more or less absolute. If the text must be continued, i.e. the account given stops short, then there is little close control of what the student will write. A further alternative is to ask the student to produce an alternative text, e.g. 'Look at this picture. Mrs X, the lady with the dog, wrote the following letter to her sister describing the incident from her point of view. We all tend to see life from our own point of view. Write an account as if you were the man on the bicycle, etc.'

In this case the language patterns and lexis used by the lady with a dog might be manipulated only slightly to produce a very different account.

Example 1

Fig. 33

This is a strip cartoon made by boys for a teacher. It was made by cutting up a comic, by remounting the drawings and by photocopying the result. The pupils may either write their text and dialogue on the strip or in their books. Useful patterns and lexis could be given.

The choice of a strip depends on availability, on interest level, and on the possibility of control.

Example 2   (From Boothman, Book 1, Further reading 5)

Study these three drawings which show the Unwin family breaking some of the country code. In the spaces opposite each drawing briefly explain what might happen. Add a fourth of your own, using the clues on the opposite page.

Complete the moral : _____ the _____ CODE.

Fig. 34

The pupils could also be asked to write a protest letter to the newspaper about the behaviour of people from the towns, to write notices which might be put up to correct bad behaviour in the country, to write down what a farmer might say if he were to phone the police to complain, to write down what the farmer might say if he spoke to the family.

Example 3   A visitor is coming from abroad to stay with you and your family. With the help of this map and bus timetable write to explain how to get to your home. Apologise to him and explain that you can't be at the station to meet him.

The teacher should use an actual map of the student's home town or region.

Unguided composition

Many of the points discussed under Speaking Composition apply equally here. The examples given could also be used for writing composition. In the examples below the writing activity is not merely an alternative to speaking composition, nor a preparation for it. I have tried to choose examples in which writing is in fact the mode that a native speaker might use in the same situation.

Example 1   With the aid of maps, photographs, a list of events, list of trades and professional services, graphs showing types of employment or weather, write a guide to your village, town or region for foreign visitors.

Example 2   Choose a private advertisement from a newspaper or magazine from the foreign country and write a letter asking for further information about it, describing your own particular needs if this is relevant. This could be a real rather than simulated exercise.

Students might also write to tourist offices in the foreign country asking for literature or to societies in the foreign country who are following the same line of interest as the student himself. They might also join in a correspondence argument going on in a newspaper in the foreign country.

Example 3   With the support of photographs, drawings and maps, write a short autobiography. Alternatively, keep a diary.

Example 4   The village as it used to be and the village as it is today. Contrasted pictures often stimulate ideas. A few of the ways of using these two pictures are given below.

Students write: − the sort of letter the old lady might send to relatives abroad describing how the village has changed since she was a little girl;
− a report about the changes in the village and the need for new traffic control regulations;
− letters by the students addressed to a local newspaper comparing the 'old days' with today.
(See Fig. 35.)

Fig. 35

Example 5   In   Edward   de   Bono's   *The   Dog-Exercising   Machine,*
(Penguin 1971), there are about 70 inventions devised by children for
exercising dogs. The inventions are drawn and labelled and in many cases
described.

Set a problem which has a chance of catching the fancy of the students.
They will almost inevitably want to use language to explain aspects
impossible to convey by drawing; labelling of parts, mechanics, sequence
of events, examples of usefulness, discussion of implications for society.

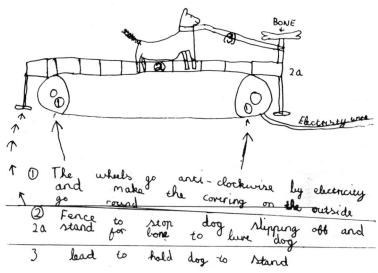

A MACHINE TO ~~ExiБ~~ EXERCISE A DOG

① The wheels go anti-clockwise by electricity
and make the covering on ~~the~~ outside
go round

② Fence to stop dog to lure slipping off and
2a stand for bone dog

3 lead to hold dog to stand

BONE

2a

~~Electricity wire~~

Fig. 36

Example 6 A totally different example of visual material which helps the student 'write' productively is the sentence maker illustrated in Fig. 67. Words known to the learner are supplied to him on separate cards. He composes sentences according to his own ideas or to a stimulus the teacher might give him. He is engaged in writing in so far as he is composing sentences with the written word. If the work of physically forming letter shapes and of spelling is likely to interfere with the act of making sentences then there is a lot to be said for using the sentence maker. It is a pity if learners are deprived of the possibility of writing productively merely because of these only partially relevant problems.

5 Grammar

Broad functions of visual materials used for the teaching of grammar

1 To clarify the meaning of a grammatical point for the pupils and to draw their attention to the precise form of the language involved.

2 For the diagrammatic analysis of text.

3 In the making of general statements about grammar.

4 To assist the pupils in their practice of the use of grammatical points.

These four points form the sub-sections of this chapter.

I Clarification

Examples which clarify the meaning of the text and draw the pupils' attention to the precise form of the language.

Contrast

Very often the easiest way of directing the pupils' understanding of the use of different tenses and the change of form necessary to show those differences is to *contrast* them. It is usually better to contrast various periods from the same on-going event than to contrast two quite different events.

Ici, un jour, il y aura un accident

Il y a un accident

Il y a eu un accident

There will be an accident. **There is an accident.** **There was an accident.**

Fig. 37

Affirmative and negative forms can be most easily compared if the same verb is used in both cases.

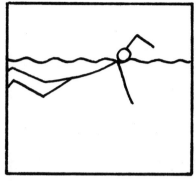

John can swim.　　　　　Mary can't swim.

Fig. 38

A number of examples

It may not always be possible to draw attention to the form of a grammatical feature through *contrast*. An alternative or even an additional help is to give a number of examples of it.

If you break this window,　If he falls,
you will have to pay for it!　he will hurt himself.

Fig. 39

2 Analysis

The diagrammatic analysis of text

To draw the attention of the students to certain features of a text the teacher or the materials producer can use colour, e.g. coloured letters, heavy type, underlining and boxing. An important technique when comparing and contrasting language texts is to position the key points to invite comparison.

　　　　You saw it.
　　　Did you see it?
rather than
　　　You saw it. Did you see it?

The overhead projector is a most useful instrument for the analysis of texts by students or teacher. (See Media)

3 General statements

Example 1
(Acknowledgement is made to ELT Documents, The British Council (73/2))
'It's possible to work out your own scheme to cover all the tenses, e.g.

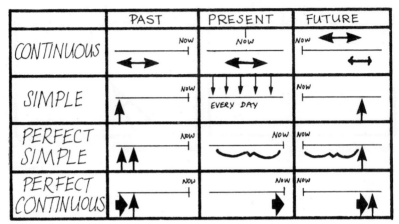

Fig. 40

I Listening comprehension

Notes:

1   The above tells nothing like the whole story – e.g.

i   Future Continuous form used with a one-moment concept ('We'll be leaving at 6.0' – not a period, but an action regarded as an activity) isn't catered for;

ii   Present/Past-Continuous special use with *ALWAYS* stressing recurrence;

iii   Past-Simple used to register past habit.

2   However, by juxtaposing two of these very simple diagrams, one can illustrate differences in tense concepts, or similarities; e.g.

i   Contrast the two lines for Past Simple + Present Perfect to reinforce the idea of *DEFINITE/INDEFINITE* past time;

ii   Superimpose the lines for Past-Simple and Past-Continuous and you can represent the interruption of the second by the first;

iii   Compare the diagrams for the three Perfect-Continuous tenses and you get quite a satisfying parallel concept.'

(Worth noting incidentally that even the direction of the line is debatable – is future left-to-right or vice versa?)

Doug Case who wrote the article, 'Visual Reminders for Structures' from which this extract is taken qualifies the implications inherent in the diagram above. Such diagrams are of interest and many others are shown in his article. However, there is a danger in their use which is indicated by the qualifications in the article. It is easy for the student to conclude that, just as the various tense forms can be used in the way shown, so each time reference can only be described by those tense forms. This would, of course, be untrue.

Example 2 A grammar correction box

Bright and McGregor (see Further reading 6) suggest that the individual correction of pupils is easy provided that the explanations and exercises are put on cards and indexed instead of being written on the blackboard or in a pupil's book. It is suggested that the explanation and examples be put on one side of the card and the exercises on the other.

There is a lot to be said for making these cards attractive to the student in the grammatical examples. Humour or information or experiments might provide this type of interest.

This suggested use of visual materials adds to administrative convenience.

4 Practice

The grammatical table, both the drawn version (Fig. 16) and the push and pull model (Fig. 56) and the grammatical roll (Fig. 17), all give concentrated practice in the use of certain sentence patterns. At the same time the visual draws the attention of the student to the features of the pattern he is using.

Further reading 16

6 Testing

Testing is an increasingly refined aspect of language teaching. Valette (Further Reading 7.8) and others distinguish carefully between various types of test and their sub-divisions. These sub-divisions include techniques of establishing the pupils' achievement in individual skills. Within each skill one can further test the understanding of single discrete items, or on the other hand, test the pupils' ability in guided narration or in free composition.

The main contribution of visuals to testing is summarised below under 'Broad functions . . . . . .'

What sort of style is appropriate for visuals used in testing? The amount of information given in visuals and the style of it, *must* be determined by its function. Visuals used to test the students' understanding of single items will probably contain only sufficient information for the object, action or situation to be recognised. On the other hand, visuals intended to stimulate the pupil to talk or write freely might well give a mass of information interpretable in a variety of ways. (Of course this type of test is not a 'strict' test; there is no basis for comparison between pupil and pupil or pupil and criterion.) The presentation and style might be chosen to be attractive and stimulating.

In other cases the teacher might like to see whether the student can 'survive' in a real life situation. As the pupil cannot be taken to the foreign country for the test the 'real' life' conditions must be simulated in the classroom. This is mainly a matter of presenting a lot of visual and aural information to see if the pupil can sort out the relevant bits. A complex drawing, a photograph or movie film could provide the vehicle for this.

Another factor which may affect the choice of style in the visual may be the wish of the examiner to lighten the examination atmosphere a little.

All visuals should be pre-tested. It is very useful to pre-test the visuals with students of similar age and intelligence in both the target language and the mother tongue. Tests in the mother tongue are a way of testing the interpretation of the pictures by the students. The teacher may then replace or modify a picture. At least he will be forewarned about those which are confusing.

Many of the following examples were developed by the Testing Section of the Schools Council Languages Project in York and used by the Oxford Examination Board.

Broad functions of the use of visual materials for testing

1 To avoid the use of text by the examiner in order that the student derive the answer from a selection of language from his memory.

2 To reduce the number of decisions and actions involving language not directly relevant to the feature being tested e.g. testing listening comprehension by indicating an appropriate picture instead of speaking or writing an answer which is a test of these skills as well as that of listening.

3 To stimulate the examinee's own ideas and to give him things to talk about.

4 To give a real life context to the test without the provision of any specific information.

Example 1   To test the students' ability to discriminate and recognise the meaning indicated by certain phonemes within an utterance.
In picture 1 there is a boy eating an ice cream. In picture 2 there is an apple in a boy's hand. Only in picture 3 is a boy shown eating an apple. The pupil must, therefore, understand the complete sentence in order to choose picture 3.

Example 2   To test the students' ability to understand short statements. Nine small pictures are shown to the student (three only are illustrated here). The student listens and indicates each picture as he hears the

Fig. 41

corresponding sentence. Note, if only two pictures are shown the pupil has a 50% chance of getting the correct picture based on luck! Nine pictures reduce luck to a minimum and provide, economically, an extensive test. If the pictures are all depicting aspects of the same topic, then guesswork is further reduced as the student must understand all the information in order to decide on the appropriate picture. If the pictures were quite different, he would merely need to understand a bit of the statement in order to decide which it was.

Example 3   To test undirected extensive listening for gist.
Four picture strips are given each representing a short *sentence* of events.
    The examinee listens and indicates the appropriate strip.

Fig. 42

These situations and picture sequences are fairly easy to devise for simple structures and concrete vocabulary. They are not so easy to devise for later stages.

The test can be made more difficult by adding information in the pictures not directly relevant to the text.

Example 4 To test undirected intensive listening for detail. The examinee looks at a picture containing a number of actions, relationships and objects. Statements are made about the picture. The examinee indicates which statements are true and which are false.

Fig. 43

Example 5 To test undirected intensive listening for detail.

Four drawings or photographs of different professional or trades people are shown. A taped statement is played to the examinee. He indicates the drawing of the person he thinks is connected with the statement.

Fig. 44

Similarly four pictures of different scenes are shown. A dialogue is played to the examinee. He indicates the picture he feels is associated with that dialogue.

Example 6 To test undirected intensive listening for detail.

A map or a scene is described on tape. The pupil sketches it. Alternatively simple instructions are given and the pupil colours in a drawing as directed.

2 Speaking

Example 1 Questions based on pictures

1 The teacher will begin by asking the candidate a number of set questions on pictures. These questions will require the candidate to use descriptive language and will not have been prepared by the candidate beforehand.

2 This situation will lead on to personal questions. Here the teacher will not be asked to adhere rigidly to a number of set questions, but will be encouraged to develop a genuine (although brief) conversation.

In the 1971 examination each candidate was examined using five pictures out of a total number of eight e.g.

Fig. 45

Text of questions

1 What is the woman doing?
2 What is the weather like?
3 What is the weather going to be like very soon?

General Questions e.g. What sort of weather do you prefer?
          Why?
          What do you wear in wet weather?

Example 2   Narration of a story based on a sequence of pictures.
In this section the candidate will be required to use narrative language.
He will be given a short time for preparation.
    The following instruction was issued to teachers –
    'At the start of this section of the examination the examiner will give
the candidate one of the oral narratives to prepare. He should warn the
candidate that he will be asked to narrate the story told by the pictures, in
the *Present Tense.*
    . . . . In order to start the candidate talking, some simple openings to
each narrative are suggested below. These may be varied slightly if the
examiner wishes. Once the candidate has started, the examiner should
intervene as little as possible. This section is not intended as a question-
and-answer exercise, and so questions from the examiner should be used
sparingly, i.e. only when he feels that they are essential to maintain the
flow of conversation.'

Suggested openings

1 Now you are going to tell me about the story of the fire. Who arrives?
2 Now tell me the story of the outing in the car.

3 Writing

Example 1   Pictures can be used in tests which call for the student to
produce single items. (cf. Further reading 78)

 What's this?

It's a . . . .

 What's he doing?

He's . . . .

 The cat is . . . . . the table.

For more complex items it is often necessary to give written as well
as pictorial aids.

 John is big but his mother is . . . .

Example 2

Questions based on pictures (from Micklegale Newsletter Schools Council Modern Languages Project, York, No. 3, 1972.)

'This section is designed to look more precisely at command of structure and lexis than, for example, the picture composition. It does not claim to be an objective test, confining candidates to one possible answer. There will nearly always be some variety of response possible within the terms of the question. By using a variety of stimuli, the examiner can sample widely from within the language syllabus. e.g.

Fig. 46

1 Who is at the table in the restaurant?	1 What is the young woman doing?
2 What is there on the tables?	2 What did the little boy do when his photograph was taken?

Example 3 A composition based on a series of pictures

'The aim of this section is to test candidates' ability to write a connected flow of language on a simple narrative theme, outlined by a series of pictures.

The theme of the picture composition was the simple one of the lost-found variety entitled "The Lost Purse" and told in a series of eight pictures,

The following is the rubric from the 1971 paper:

'Write in French, in not less than 110 words and not more than 130 words, the story of "The Lost Purse", told in the series of pictures below. Use past tenses."

Example 4

The aim of this section is to test the candidate's knowledge of the cultural background.Candidates were asked to choose one of three questions, each referring to a photograph, and to write 30-50 words in English. e.g.   10. In which city or cities in Spain would you see scenes like that depicted in picture B, and at what time of year? Why are the people wearing a costume and why are they carrying a cross?'

Further reading 78

7 Culture

Not all teachers and their students are concerned with the culture of the native speakers of the language they are learning. The cultural background in English speaking countries can have little relevance to the Indian engineer intent on reading books on engineering, to the sailor or airman using English for navigation, to the African or Indian using English as a lingua franca. This chapter is, therefore, primarily for those teachers who do have an element of cultural information as one of their aims.

Broad functions of visual materials used for the teaching of cultural information

1 To make the foreign country and culture credible to the student.

2 To interest the student.

3 To give him information.

4 To cause him to compare and contrast features of the foreign culture with his own.

5 To help him to recognise visual features of the behaviour of the people in order to interpret this behaviour correctly and to use it appropriately himself.

There is not usually enough time in a language course to give this varied experience of the foreign culture unless every opportunity is taken. Cultural information can be conveyed by all the visual material used in a language course. A variety of physical and facial types, a variety of ages, people from different social groupings, different physical behaviour, variety of cars, houses, towns, etc., can be illustrated in the material intended for language learning activities. Of course, very often the element of cultural authenticity must be subdued in order not to distract the student from the language learning. The element of cultural information must be judged according to the aims and circumstances of each situation.

The examples below are grouped firstly according to materials for developing the appreciation of the geography, history and social character of the foreign country, and secondly according to materials for the more practical and immediate knowledge and skills necessary for survival in the foreign country.

I Appreciation

Example 1 In this section, as in the rest of the book, I have tried to give examples which involve media which are readily available, controllable and/ or easy to manufacture by the teacher. However, in the case of the appreciation of the culture of the foreign country it would be difficult to leave out film. Whereas in so much language work one is concerned with carefully controlling the amount of visual information, in developing appreciation of the culture every aspect of visual experience should be available. Qualities of light, colour, space, form and movement often become all-important. So, too, does sound; the intonation patterns of different localities or the quietness of a cricket match.

Tourist films are not usually appropriate for language teaching. It is perhaps a reasonable generalisation that holidays are mainly used as an escape from the normal. Tourist films stress the unusual, the quaint and the irresponsible. The films produced specifically for language teaching are very different. Mary Glasgow has produced a number of colour sound films of this sort.

The film of *Entrechaux* covers a day in the life of the village, with stress on vine growing and wine making. '. . . . . the material can be used in a simple way to describe daily life in France. All the elements are there: the café, the town hall, the baker's shop, the grocer's, the post office, the church and the school. The people go about their work and play or pass the time of the day in chat. No film actors are used.'

Fig. 47 Stills from 'Entrechaux'

The reality and the obvious authenticity of this film do not encourage the viewer to make shallow generalisations. The stress is on the individuality of the village and its people. The film is part of a kit which includes a filmstrip of stills from the film and teacher's notes.

The advantage of the still pictures is that the students can concentrate on the details of shops, streets, houses and clothes.

Example 2   This is an example of modest teacher-made material. Picture and text are pasted down onto individual cards. Questions are pasted on the back of a folded flap which can be brought forward to cover the text. It is probably most satisfying to the student if the card is big and at least one of the pictures a generous size. Transparent self sealing film will protect the card and give it a 'professional' look.

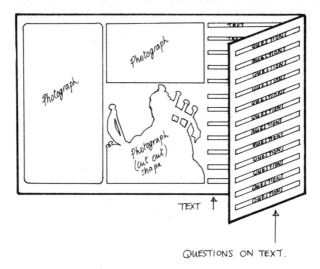

QUESTIONS ON TEXT.   **Fig. 48**

Example 3   A bulletin board can have something of the character of a magazine. It might show cuttings from newspapers of the target culture, cartoons and strip drawings, interesting advertisements, poems and pictures, also news about the school itself and holidays mapped out and described. In the texts contributed by the pupil repeated mistakes should be marked in some way. However, the texts should not be too heavily corrected as the event will appear to be yet another trick by the teacher to exact work from the pupils. There is also some considerable justification for leaving in the mistakes to convince the pupils that their level of achievement in the foreign language is enough for basic understanding. Alternatively the display might concentrate on a single theme. In either case the display should be attractively conceived (for layout see How to do it page 133) and changed as often as possible. It's much better to leave it empty for a week or two than to leave up 'old' material.

Example 4 The student can be caused to interact with the material, to experience it, and to make his own observations on it in a variety of ways. Three examples of this are given here:

a)

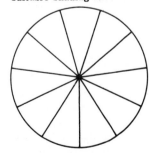

Fig. 49

These photographs show an Austrian, a German, a Russian, a Peruvian and a Frenchman.

Which is which?

b)

This circle represents the population of the United Kingdom (55 million).
It is divided into eleven segments, each representing 5 million people. Using suitable shading show how the population is divided between the four countries.

KEY		
England	46 million	
Wales	3 million	
Scotland	5 million	
N. Ireland	1 million	

Fig. 50

Of course most students could remember the 4 figures if they wanted to. Why then go to the trouble of asking them to fill in a diagram? In the act of transposing the figures to visually related segments the student is more likely to 'experience' and get a sense of the proportions than if he were merely given the figures.

The example given here does not demand very much of the student. The principle, however, of making him compare, contrast, transpose or make generalisations can be employed at any level. Teaching need not imply telling.

c)

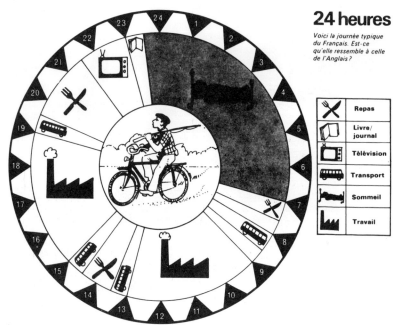

24 heures

Voici la journée typique du Français. Est-ce qu'elle ressemble à celle de l'Anglais?

✕	Repas
◫	Livre/ journal
▭	Télévision
▦	Transport
▭	Sommeil
▲	Travail

Fig. 51

Here is the typical day of a French working man.
Does it resemble that of an . . . . . . ?

To give some interesting background information and to revise the present tense of certain common verbs and the use of times.

The pupils should be given a few minutes to study '24 hours' . . . They should then talk about it, e.g. say how long the average French working man spends reading, sleeping etc. each day; how long he there- fore spends reading, sleeping, etc. each week; how long he and his family spend reading, sleeping etc. each week; know at what time he and his family get up, leave for school and work, eat, go to bed, etc. It should be pointed out here that the dangers of over-simplifying and generalising about the French are balanced to some degree in this course by filmstrip studies of the daily life of individuals.

2 'Survival knowledge'

Example 1   Portrait of a village

Gestures and facial expressions convey meaning; they are not just nervous twitchings. Shaking hands, kissing, standing up for certain people, order of introductions, the use of the right hand instead of the left for certain purposes are conventions which, when misunderstood or ignored, may create hard feeling.

The best media in which to represent those features is colour movie film or television. Still pictures cannot convey the interplay of these movements: i.e. how one person's action follows or overlaps with another's nor how any one action is performed as a complete movement. For example, shaking hands may be by a single up and down movement or by a long clasping of the hand. A still photograph could not distinguish between these various forms.

Example 2   Still photographs probably serve better than film when movement is not a key feature. For example, road signs, instructions for the use of the telephone, what to do if you lose something, or if you fall ill or have a road accident.

Phone up and ask!!

TO MAKE A CALL

Have money ready 2p or 10p
Lift receiver
Listen for continuous purring
Dial number or code and number
When you hear rapid pips press in a coin.
To continue a dialled call put in more money
during conversation or when you hear rapid
pips again.

Fig. 52   A teacher-made workcard

The photograph of the telephone box will help the foreigner to recognise one when he sees it. The labelled close-up of the telephone will familiarise him with the operation of it.

Example 3   Under the heading visual materials for 'survival' in the foreign country, one should include as many examples of objects and printed materials as possible. Tickets, programmes, telegram forms, advertisements, police fines, timetables etc.

These objects will be wasted if treated as museum curios. They should be introduced within a relevant theme, handled and referred to by the students in the knowledge of who made them for whom, when and for what purpose. Ideally, circumstances should be credibly simulated in the classroom so that the material can be used in a realistic role-playing situation, thus giving the students training in their actual use.

Further reading for Part One 2, 4, 8, 15, 27, 42, 44, 49, 52, 54, 55, 57, 58, 60, 61, 73, 79

PART TWO: Media

Introduction

Language teaching is a collective title for a variety of activities undertaken by different people in very different circumstances. There is consequently no single medium 'ideal for language teaching' as is so often claimed. The discussion in the previous section and this following one should make this very clear. In Part Two generalisations are made about the characteristics of media and the teaching for which these characteristics might be helpful. However, these are only generalisations and are at times very summary indeed.

The technical side of media is barely covered here for two reasons. Firstly there is literature available already and, secondly, information on media is often out of date before publication. Reviews in the Press or information from the producer are more reliable.

Each chapter is divided according to a brief indication of what the heading refers to; to a description of features as they relate to the language teacher; to a discussion of the significance of these features; to examples given and finally to design tips if they are peculiar to the medium. Most design tips are relevant to a variety of media and are given in How to do it and Perception.

Below is an explanation of the points in the sub-section headed, 'Description'. The reader will need to refer back to this list.

1 THE SIZE(S) OF THE NORMAL IMAGE i.e. the area of text or picture is given. This is significant in affecting how far away people can be, i.e. the size of the group.
2 THE VISUAL ELEMENTS (see Perception) What the medium can convey in terms of colour, tone, line etc. and how this might affect the sort of representational convention used; for example, diagrams, colour photographs etc.
3 MOVEMENT OR CHANGE By movement, I mean an *apparently* continuous movement. By change, I mean the representation of selected stages of a movement.
4 SOUND Whether or not sound can be technically sychronised or linked in some way with the medium.
5 AVAILABILITY How easy it is to get. How much it costs.

6 TEACHER'S AND/OR PUPIL'S CONTROL How much control the individual has over the above features.

7 CONVENIENCE Handling, storage etc.

I Blackboards, whiteboards

In the U.S. blackboards are more reasonably called chalkboards. More reasonably, because they are often green! The main characteristic is the use of chalk. In contrast, whiteboards have very smooth surfaces, on which water based felt tip pens are used. Note: some whiteboards have the properties of the magnet board (see page 70). All whiteboards can be used as screens for projection purposes.

Description

1 Sizes vary greatly.

2 Generally speaking, only line is used. The representational conventions resulting from this are text, diagrams and pinmen.

3 Change can be shown by adding to, removing or substituting part of the image; for example, composite drawings can be made and changed in this way.

4 —

5 The most common and inexpensive of equipment.

6 The teacher has good control over the use of this equipment. However, there are difficulties, for example, in making a number of texts or complicated drawings suddenly appear – cf. the overhead projector.

7 There are few technical or storage problems. In the language laboratory the dust of the chalk spoils the tapes. (Whiteboards are better in this respect.)

Discussion

There is much talk of the overhead projector having replaced the chalkboard; it has not and will not. Chalkboards and whiteboards are cheap and involve no technical problems. The whiteboard is probably more useful than the chalkboard, particularly if it has magnetic properties, so that prepared material can be quickly displayed.

Examples See Figs. 10, 23

Design

There is a tendency for teachers to make sketchy drawings on the blackboard. Lines should be bold and strong to ensure visibility and to convey conviction. Writing and drawing should be big and simple. Sketchy flicks and other mannerisms are confusing and time-consuming.

By standing to the left of the board the right-handed teacher is less likely to obscure his own work.

The teacher may want to make a fairly complicated drawing or a sequence of drawings on the blackboard. It is easy, at this time, to get carried away and to forget the class, which rapidly gets out of control or bored. If it is not possible to prepare the drawing beforehand, then every opportunity should be taken as the drawing is made to get the students to talk about it. Even such simple questions as, 'What's this?'. What's this going to be?'. 'What do you think will happen next?' will all help to keep the attention of the class and provide valuable practice work.

Further reading 20

2 Overhead projector

This equipment projects horizontally placed transparencies on to a screen without any darkening of the room. Several transparencies can be placed together to form a single image. The transparencies can be drawn on during projection.

Description

1 The size of the projected image averages 3 sq. metres, which is satisfactory for even large lecture rooms.
2 Line, tone and colour can be shown. However, for technical reasons, it is not usually possible to show photographs and other graded tonal images.
3 A simple mechanical movement of the image is possible. However, 'change' can be shown in the image projected by means of the over-laying of further transparencies.
4 —
5 Overhead projectors cost approximately £70-£100. They are increasingly common in secondary and further education in Britain. However, they are not usually found in language teaching departments.
   The transparencies are easily written and drawn on by the teacher while the lesson is in progress. Alternatively, they may be pre-prepared. Transparencies can be made from printed material on some photocopying machines. There are very few published transparencies for language teaching.
6 The teacher can easily control what appears on the screen, thus focusing and directing the students' attention. The teacher can mask out parts of the image merely by placing a piece of paper over the part of the transparency he wishes to obscure.
   Being able to pre-prepare his material and to limit its presentation allows the teacher to control the medium very successfully.
7 There are few technical problems. The transparencies are easy to store.

Discussion

The overhead projector is of great potential help to the language teacher, in particular, giving the opportunity of pre-preparing complex textual or pictorial material and of controlling its presentation. Students can write or draw on the transparency material which can then be projected and discussed.

The fact that the teacher faces the class while using the overhead projector is a great help in language teaching. The noise of the cooling fans of some models is a disadvantage.

It is ideal for the language laboratory. It gives a big image, attention is controlled, there is no dust and if it is well positioned, the teacher need not leave his console.

Examples

Example 1
Picture story sequence

Six stages in a story sequence. The bus, man, garage door move by being slid along on the surface of the transparency.

Fig. 53   Use of silhouettes – cut out paper, toy cars, toy running man

Example 2
Homonyms and spelling

1   Basic
    transparency

2   **Basic transparency**
    + 1st overlay

3   **Basic transparency**
    + 2nd overlay

Fig. 54

Example 3
The revealing wheel

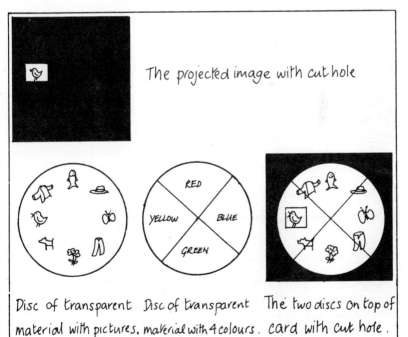

Fig. 55   This principle can be used for text and pictures or text alone

Example 4
Substitution tables

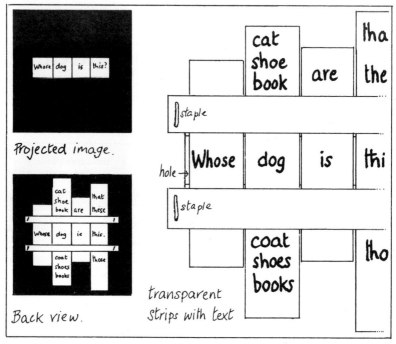

Fig. 56

Design

Technical advice and simple tips on the preparation of transparencies are given in the handbooks which go with the machine. There are also several excellent books giving more detailed advice. Some of these books are cheap to buy and easily obtainable.

Further reading 65, 67, 70

3 Magnet board, flannelgraph board, plastigraph

All three devices act as supports for the display of pictures, single cut out figures or objects.

Description

1 The size should be as big as possible. 1 m x 1.25 m is probably adequate for class use.
2 Published material is usually brightly coloured which helps visibility. A naturalistic artist's style is less useful than a very simple and bold representation.

3 Change can be shown by the addition, subtraction or transference of pictures and parts of pictures; for example, people or words can be added. Figures can be jointed and thus demonstrate a variety of actions.

4 –

5 All three media are easily obtainable. The flannelgraph is the cheapest to buy or to make. The pictures and words displayed on these supports are also easy to make.

6 The teacher has excellent control over the visual material presented to the student. In the case of magnet board he can draw with chalk if it is a dark surface or with pen if it is a white surface. He thus combines pre-prepared pictures and words with 'spontaneous' pictures, diagrams, symbols and words.

7 The flannelgraph and the plastigraph are easy to store and light to handle. The magnet board is heavier. There are no technical problems with any of them.

There can be some problem over the storage and retrieval of the pictures and words. If there are a great many it may be difficult for the teacher to find the ones he needs. The solution lies largely in lesson planning.

Adhesion is best on magnet board, worst on flannelgraph, with plastigraph somewhere between the two.

Discussion

Which medium is the best? A difficult question. The magnet board is heavy but the adhesion is good and the possibility of drawing on the board is useful. The plastigraph is light and figures adhere well when clean. On the other hand, it is more difficult for the teacher to display any picture he may find because of the need for a smooth plastic surface. The flannelgraph does not give such good adhesion and it is slightly more bother for the teacher to adapt any picture for use (e.g. to give it a flocked or a sandpaper backing or whatever is appropriate). On the other hand, it is the cheapest system.

Vocabulary teaching and simple dialogues are often aided by these media.

Concrete nouns and simple actions can be well represented. Some adjectives and prepositions are also easily shown. However, abstract and subtle qualities are usually quite impossible to represent or suggest.

Manipulative work goes well with these media as words and/or pictures can be substituted in basic sentence patterns.

The possibility of having pre-prepared words means that sentences can be formed without the mechanical involvement of writing. The sentences can be linked with pictures or can label them.

The possibility of making sentences with pre-prepared words and of substituting parts of these sentences encourages the student to make generalisations about the language. Symbols and diagrams can be used to demonstrate grammatical analysis.

The fact that the words and pictures are physical, tangible objects, encourages younger children particularly to take part and to actually manipulate the pictures and words themselves.

Examples

Example 1   Picture for question and answer work or storytelling

Fig. 57

Example 2   Subject, predicate and qualifiers

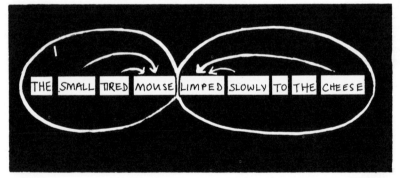

Fig. 58

Pre-prepared word cards combined with the teacher's use of chalk lines draw attention to parts of the sentence.

Other examples

1   Individual letters for spelling. Note these can be easily bought for the magnet board.
2   Sentence making.
3   Sentence substitution and sentence study.
4   Labelling of pictures with pre-prepared words.

5 Pictures, perhaps in sequences, for story making or as a cue for the reproduction of dialogues.
6 Picture scenes for question and answer work.
7 Division of the support area for the purposes of drawing attention to, for example, gender categories or sentence formation.

Further reading 10

4 Flashcards

Cards printed with words and/or pictures which· can be handled easily by the teacher.

Description

1 Sizes vary according to the picture or text shown. Basically they are of a size easy for the teacher to handle and to flash at the pupils.
2 Text, line, tone and colour may be printed or drawn by the teacher. A simple and bold use of these elements will carry most clearly over a distance and make most impact. Both sides of the flash card can be used.
3 –
4 –
5 There are a number of published sets of flash cards on the market. They are also easy to make.
6 As a medium they give considerable teacher control. The teacher can prepare exactly what he wants and can show the material either in isolation or with other visuals when he chooses.
7 They are easy to handle and to store. There are no technical problems. The card must, of course, be strong enough not to bend and flop.

Discussion

Flash cards are suitable for the pictorial representation of single concepts, for example, of actions or of objects. They are not so good for the introduction of new items of language if the teacher believes in introducing new items in a story, dialogue or other textual context. Flash cards are most suitable for the revision of known language and for recombination or manipulation work, the picture or word acting as a cue for substitution. The size and shape of the card are excellent for speedy and stimulating work. The total absence of technical problems means they can be used easily for short periods of time.

Examples

Example 1 Phonological practice
Each card shows one person – perhaps a funny depiction – whose name contains the sound to be practised. Alternatively, cards illustrating, e.g. *day, baker, grey, lake, page.*

Example 2   Word Cards for Sentence Making (Fig. 67)
These can be propped up in a stand. Alternatively, pupils, each equipped
with a word card, can so arrange themselves that they show a sentence
to the rest of the class.

Example 3   Reading recognition
Each pupil is given a word or a sentence card and must indicate an object
or scene in the room or in a picture to which it relates. Alternatively, the
card contains an instruction which the pupil carries out.

Example 4   Reading recognition
Question cards and appropriate answer cards are mixed. The pupil or group
of pupils must sort them out and match them.

Example 5   Relating written and spoken forms

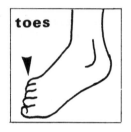

Fig. 59

Example 6   Weather

Fig. 60

Example 7   Countable nouns, uncountable nouns

Fig. 61

Example 8   Tenses
What is he doing? What was he doing?
The teacher shows the flash card picture, establishes what the person is
doing and then hides it. He then asks, 'What was he doing?'.

Fig. 62

Example 9   Guessing game
The teacher shows a number of cards of actions to the class. First he asks
them to remember the pictures; then he picks one up, conceals the picture
and asks them to say what it is — perhaps pretending to try out the pupils'
powers of extra-sensory perception. Each pupil makes a guess. Then the
teacher looks at the card he has taken and asks each pupil again, 'what did
you say?'

Example 10   Contrasts for meaning
Flash cards with pictures on both sides can be used to reinforce the recognition of contrasting concepts and to give oral reproduction practice.
(Fig. 38)
   a He can swim. She can't swim.
      Can you swim? No I can't.
   b He has a dog. She hasn't got a dog.
      Have you got a dog? No I haven't.
   c He likes chocolate. She doesn't like chocolate.
Other features of the target language may be contrasted, for example:
phonological similarity and written dissimilarity.

5 Wallcharts, wallposters, wallpictures

Wallcharts illustrate aspects of a topic, for example, 'The British Constitu-
tion', in both textual and pictorial terms. On one chart use may be made of
photograph, artist's drawing, symbol, graph and text.

Wallposters illustrate a limited bit of information. They are used in advertising and propaganda. In language teaching they may be used to represent
single actions or objects, they may also be part of a sequence of pictures.

Wallpictures represent subjects containing a mass of information. These may be composite wallpictures, meant by the publisher to be used for language work, or cultural information pictures, as supplied by Tourist Boards.

Description

1 There is no ideal size for any of these media. The size depends on what is to be shown and on convenience.

2 Published versions are usually in full colour. It is not a *technical* problem for the teacher to colour his own charts etc, but it is a visual design problem. The style adopted, naturalistic, diagrammatic etc. should be decided on the basis of the content, visibility and the students' interests and expectations.

3 Change is shown by related sequences of images, either on one sheet, for example, four pictures illustrating a short story, or alternatively by four separate pictures.

4 Sequences of pictures are usually accompanied by taped dialogue. Charts of text may also have a linked tape.

5 There are a number of published, composite wallpictures and sequences of wallpictures available. The relatively high cost of these tempts the teacher to squeeze more out of them than the pupils are naturally interested in giving!

Some types of wallchart, poster and picture are relatively easy for the teacher to make. (See How to do it.)

6 The teacher's control over these media is reasonable, but certainly not absolute. He has no means, other than by pointing, of controlling what the pupil looks at. (Contrast the single object or action on the flash card.) Also, these media are usually bought by the teacher and thus not designed exactly according to his students' needs.

7 Wallcharts, posters and pictures are not easy to store and to handle by reason of their size and flimsiness.

Discussion

Wallcharts   These are not so much for class as for small group or individual student use. Hence the content need not be visible from the back of the classroom. Charts with text and pictures have the qualities of the encyclopaedia and can be used for reference and study involving reading and writing. Questions may be given and answers sought on the chart. It is a medium unexploited by the language teacher probably through the problem of finding suitable examples. Any teacher-made chart will involve time and effort, of course. However, one way of making a chart at the right level of sophistication in subject and presentation would be to take a chart published for other purposes and to cover the text with a substitute text in the foreign language at the level the teacher feels is appropriate. (See Fig. 63 and Appendix 3.)

Wallposters   These are principally for oral-aural work. Sequences of posters are used for the presentation of taped dialogue, for listening comprehension

RNLI

How the Life-boat Service works NUMBER 2

a rescue

1 THE SIGNAL

If you were at the seaside and saw a man firing two rockets into the sky would you know why? It probably means someone at sea is in trouble and the life-boat is going out to help. The rockets soar high into the sky leaving a trail of smoke after exploding into a green star with a resounding bang. The rockets are called maroons, and alert the life-boat crew.

2 THE CREW

Every crew member drops what he is doing when he hears the maroons go off. They run, ride a bicycle or drive a car as fast as they can to the life-boat station. Once they arrive they quickly don their sea clothes. The man in command from the moment a life-boat puts to sea is the coxswain.

3 THE LAUNCH

The life-boat is launched down the slipway with a mighty splash. But there are other ways of launching a life-boat; sometimes the conditions are not right for a slip-way and the boat can be launched from an open beach by a special carriage and tractor, or over skids. Some boats lie afloat in harbours or estuaries. It depends on the local conditions and which method is quicker – every second counts!

4 THE SEARCH

A search for a small boat in the open sea and in rough conditions can be very difficult. Often visibility is not good and the life-boat needs the help of direction finding equipment and other navigational aids, like radar, to find a ship in trouble. Even with this modern equipment the search can often be long and hard.

5 LIFE-LINE

Once a ship in distress is sighted the real rescue begins. The life-boat crew have to be very careful going alongside another boat as it may be very dangerous and the life-boat can be badly battered. All the same the survivors have to be taken off to safety as soon as possible.

6 RESCUE

Everybody safe and sound and on their way home, wrapped in blankets and with a hot drink – thanks to the life-boat. Since the R.N.L.I. was started in 1824 life-boats have saved nearly 100,000 people. The average of lives saved is now about 25 per week!

No 2 of four educational posters issued by Duckhams Ltd. for the Royal National Life-boat Institution. For further details on the life-boat service write to P.R. Dept. R.N.L.I. 42 Grosvenor Gardens, London, SW1 0EF

Duckhams supply the lubricants for RNLI life-boats

Fig. 63

Fig. 64
'The haunted house'
from a French course for
Primary School children
(En Avant)

and to aid the grasp of meaning. Subsequently they may be used at the reproduction stage to remind the student of what to say and to provide him with a context within which to say it. Alternatively, a sequence of posters can be used to guide oral production without any model being given to the student. For all these activities, pinmen drawing is adequate if a cultural context is not essential. (See Fig. 64)

Wallpictures   Although there are published wallpictures available, I have chosen a picture produced by a teacher. The teacher, Donn Byrne of the British Council, has developed a variety of ways of exploiting this picture, which include aural comprehension exercises, structural exercises, conversational exercises; language games, opportunities for guided composition and for free expression! (See Fig. 65)

A few examples of these ideas for exploitation are listed below:

1   Aural Comprehension
A series of statements containing inaccurate information are read out by the teacher. The pupils listen, raise their hands if they notice an inaccuracy and correct it.

2   Past Progressive
Question: What was happening in the High Street at ten o'clock?

Answer: The policeman was standing at the street corner. A man was cleaning a shop window. etc.

3 Dialogue including *wear/have on:*
Student 1: What was the old woman wearing?
Student 2: A green suit.
Student 1: Did she have a hat on?
Student 2: Yes, she did.
Students create alternative dialogues using this as a model.

4 Dialogue
Student 1: Is that P.C. Smith over there?
Student 2: Where?
Student 1: Standing on this street corner.
Student 2: Yes, that's him alright.
Student 1: I thought it was.
Students create alternative dialogues referring to other people in the picture.

5 Game
One student imagines that he is' hiding somewhere in the picture. The others must ask questions to locate exactly where he is.
Question: Are you in the garage?
Answer: No.
Question: Are you in the aeroplane?
Answer: Yes!

6 Free Expression
The students are asked to speculate about the name of the village, where it is, how many people there are, what the names of the people are, what has happened to the black car, whether the yellow car belongs to the young man or not, etc, etc.

Fig. 65

7 Discussion

The students are asked to compare the advantages and disadvantages of living in a village, to say whether they would prefer to be a policeman or a window cleaner.

8 Composition

The students are asked to compare orally or in writing what one of the people in the picture might have done or might do next. The account should be made in the first person.

Pictures of this type may be drawn by making use of the drawing tips in Part Four. It is often more efficient, and certainly more amusing, if several teachers work together on the production of such pictures.

Cultural information wallpictures

These can be on permanent display and will give a general feel of 'foreign-ness' in the language classroom. However, it is almost certain that no one will ever look at the pictures in a concentrated way except possibly on first sight. It is a good idea to talk about the picture when it is first put up, what can be seen in it, how these observations relate to the student's own experience. My own view is that cultural information pictures are better shown as slides with the benefits of big, bright and colourful images or as photographs in books or on cards for inspection at leisure by the individual student.

Summary — wallcharts, wallposters, wallpictures

There are no general rules about the design and use of these media except:
  a if something is meant to be visible from the back of the class it should be!
  b the language work associated with it should, as often as possible, spring out of the interest of the student in what he sees.

Further reading 9, 21, 28

6 Tops, clocks and games

A great number of devices have been made by teachers for the primary and early secondary years of language teaching. These include the examples on page 81.

Description

  1 —
  2 These media are teacher-made, their design and form are usually bright and 'game-like'.
  3 —
  4 —

Fig. 66 These drawings represent the three types of device rather than provide examples

5 Such devices are not necessarily difficult to make although some I have seen must have taken many hours to do.

6 There is considerable control by the teacher over these media in the sense that he makes them according to his pupils' needs and introduces them at the right moment.

7 Storage can be a problem.

Discussion

Of course one associates games with children and I am sure many teachers might feel they are only appropriate for the under-twelves. Yet games of all kinds are played by adults — by choice! Are there not any games for adults which can be adapted to the language teacher's purpose?

The advantage of games and devices generally is that they make what is essentially oral reproduction and manipulation, listening comprehension and intensive reading into activities significant to the student. Furthermore, the language is used for a purpose and is an essential part of an event.

Tops, Clocks and Games are particularly relevant to group work.

Examples

Example 1   Spin the top (Fig. 66)
The segment upon which the top comes to rest provides a pictorial or verbal cue to the pupil.
In this example:-

A   Pupil 1: What is it?
         Pupil 2: It's a dog.
B   Pupil 1: What will it be?
         Pupil 2: I think it will be a cat.

Alternatively, sentences may be made with several tops, each top containing one part of a sentence. An alternative form and design is to spin a 'clock' finger until it comes to rest on one segment.

Example 2   Revolving clocks
Devices such as the clock in Fig. 66 can be designed to produce predetermined combinations of pictures or text.

In the example here the left hand side window determines the subject of the sentence and the middle window the verb and the right hand side window the object. With ten words or small drawings on each disc many different sentences can be made.

The size of this device is determined by whether it is for class use.or small group use.

Further reading 42

7 Sentence makers

There are various devices for helping the pupil to form written sentences. Some of these control the pattern and ensure that it is syntactically, if not necessarily morphologically correct.

Description
This can be summarised in saying that they are normally teacher-made devices and thus are eminently controllable by him.

Discussion
These devices need not involve the student in actual writing even though he is involved in making sentences. The fact that the words have, by the nature of the material, a physical reality will no doubt help many people who learn by handling and doing. I do not think this necessarily excludes people with high I.Q.'s.

The student can be made more conscious of the parts of the sentence pattern by colour coding of the parts or the actual labelling of them.

Examples

Example 1 A great success in *Breakthrough to Literacy* (Further reading, 59) is the 'sentence maker'. This is simply a holding device for words printed on separate pieces of card. There is no physical control over word order and no sentence is predetermined by the apparatus. The sentence maker is intended for mother tongue speakers, thus the word order is known orally by them and in reading the sentence they have made, incorrect order is apparent.

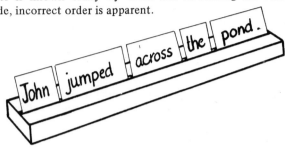

Fig. 67

Example 2 This device Fig. 56 controls the order of words and draws attention to the parts of the sentence. It is a moving version of the 'table' often reproduced in text books.

Further reading 59

8 Drama–visual materials

Definition, description and discussion
Under this heading I include objects to be used in dialogues, role playing and puppetry.

Objects Commercial packets, magazines, money, hats, bow ties, tablecloths, telephones, guns, theatre knives (the type in which the blade retracts).

Sets Large cardboard boxes, large pieces of fabric, tables, posters, time-tables. . .

Masks These are very useful for dramatic purposes, but also for hiding the shy face (if you can once get it over the shy head!).

Puppets Puppets are only likely to be accepted by primary school children: They are very successful with most children, particularly so with children too shy to act out in front of the class. However, it is not only the shy ones who gain; other children seem to welcome speaking 'through' puppets, perhaps because the inevitably limited language of beginners is often associated with puppets and, therefore, seems more natural.

Further reading 53, 69, 71

9   Realia

Definition, description and discussion

Objects The Direct Method has long involved the use of objects rather than pictures of objects. The objects can be quite ordinary things to cue oral manipulation work such as pens, books and hats, or relate to particular topics such as clocks, calendars, timetables, tickets or particular topics of interest to the pupils including their hobby collection, pets, 'finds' or 'gimmicks' including trick nails which appear to pierce the bearer's finger or ghastly plastic centipedes.

Stamps Some collections of objects can offer far more than cues for oral manipulation. Stamp collections can stimulate oral or written production on a great variety of topics. Ian F. Finlay, writing in *Modern Languages* ('Postage Stamps in Modern Language Teaching', *Modern Languages* Vol. XLIX No 3 September 1968 p119-121) made a number of interesting suggestions about the use of stamps. He says that various historical occasions connected with language are seen in stamp design, for example, the adoption of the Roman alphabet by Turkey. Stamps provide a source of various alphabets and orthography, texts and quotations, and propaganda. Stamps also represent a great amount of varied cultural information including the history of literature, inventions, geography and athletics. (See also Chapter on Culture).

10   Epidiascopes, episcopes

Epidiascopes can be used to project images both from slides and filmstrips and from opaque objects, for example, book pages or small flat objects.
    Episcopes can be used to project images from opaque objects.

Description

1   The size of the projected image will depend on the individual machine and the distance from the screen. No useful generalisation can be made.
2   Book pages, newspapers, coins, insects etc. can be shown in colour.
3   Movement cannot be shown but change, by means of successive stills from a sequence, can be.
4   Sound can be linked with slide or filmstrip. (See next section – slide and filmstrip projectors.)
5   Old models may well be easy to find in schools and colleges. However, it is the newer versions which are worth finding. New epidiascopes cost approximately £100. Episcopes are considerably less expensive.
6   The teacher has considerable control with these machines as he is able to choose from a wide variety of material. Unfortunately, use cannot be completely spontaneous as the machine must be plugged in and adjusted and the room darkened.

Discussion

Modern epidiascopes produce excellent images from a variety of material with a minimum of fuss. Old ones need a darkened room and a very white screen. They get hot, burn up books and are awkward to move. It might be the right time for language teachers to look again at the usefulness of the epidiascope in the light of new technical improvements. The only restrictions to the role of the epidiascope lie in the need for a darkened room and possible overheating. Both these points are less crucial with modern machines.

Examples

1 Cultural information can be shown, including all kinds of realia, tickets, timetables, newspapers, money.
2 Students' written work can be projected and discussed.
3 Texts can be displayed for oral reading or for singing.

II Slides and filmstrips

The most commonly published and most commonly made slide for amateurs is mounted in 5cm square mounts. Filmstrips are printed on 35 mm film.

Description

1 The size of the projected image is governed by the individual projector used and its distance from the screen. However, the picture is, potentially, very big for very little cost.
2 It is no problem to reproduce colour, line and any representational convention, drawing, photograph or text.
3 Motion cannot be shown but change can by means of related stills in sequence.
4 Sound can be linked automatically to both slides and filmstrips. An electronic pulse on the audio tape moves on the next slide or frame of the filmstrip. The equipment necessary for this arrangement is surprisingly cheap and increasingly common.

   This combination of sound and picture gives the opportunity for pre-prepared teaching kits which can be used for self-instruction.
5 Slides and filmstrips are published in great numbers for language teachers. The many sets of slides and filmstrips intended for other subjects may also prove useful to the language teacher. Slides of course are easily made by the amateur photographer.
6 Slides offer more teacher control than filmstrips. Teachers need only show the slides they are concerned with; they can intersperse their own slides with published slides; they can replace out-of-date or irrelevant slides. On some machines the slides can be projected automatically in a predetermined order. Slides can be protected from damage more easily than filmstrip. On the other hand filmstrip helps to prevent the teacher getting out of control! The order of presenta-

tion is controlled and the pictures appear the right way up. Film-strips are also cheaper and easier to store.

Both slide and filmstrip projectors can be fitted with remote control facilities. The teacher, merely by pressing a switch, can move on to the next slide or go back to the previous one.

Both slide and filmstrip projection do give the teacher a bit of bother. The room must usually be darkened, the screen prepared, the machine set up and plugged in and the slides or filmstrip fed in correctly. Spontaneous use is, therefore, difficult. It is helpful if time can be found to arrange everything before the lesson.

Discussion

Technically, anything except motion can be reproduced on slide or film-strip. The image can be big or small. The projector can be controlled by teacher or pupil. Thus, these media are used for very large groups of students or by individuals, as teacher-controlled media or as self-instructional media. Subjects taught include all the broad activity areas of the last section from colour photographic slides for cultural information to text and diagrams for grammatical analysis.

A sequence of stills is useful for the representation of steps in a process, argument, description or story. However, slides and filmstrips are not appropriate when the whole is constantly referred to and when it is necessary to make direct visual comparisons between images. In this case sequences on wallpictures, in books or by overhead projector are better. Two examples of this situation can be given. Firstly, it is helpful for young people to see all the pictures of a sequence in order to grasp the storyline as a whole rather than detail by detail. Secondly, in manipulation practice the teacher may want to show several pictures at one time to present the student with a choice.

Teachers will often want to use their own slides in the language teaching class. Perhaps the obvious should be stated. The students, even more than your family and friends, are likely to be extremely bored with your slides unless they are presented with *their* interests in mind. Furthermore, the presentation as a whole should be a reasonable bit of entertainment or have journalistic flair if cultural information is to be taught. If the slides are to be used for language teaching purposes, these purposes must be clear to the teacher and the slides appropriate in terms of the information they present to the student; for example, if the teacher intends to use photographic slides he has made in the foreign country to practise verbs of action, he may well find concentration straying to very different bits of information in the picture.

Tremendous involvement can be built up if the students themselves make tape-slide presentations.

Design

Considerations of design, letter size etc are mainly factors common to other visual media and are discussed in How to Do It. However, the one or two points below are peculiar to the preparation of artwork for slide and film-strip production which lie within the scope of the ordinary teacher.

1 The content of each frame should be kept to a minimum as there is a danger of overheating if it is projected for too long.

2 Artwork should be 18 cm x 24 cm for filmstrip (assuming single frame 18 mm x 24 mm) and 24 cm x 36 cm for slides (assuming double frame 24 mm x 36 mm) or to these proportions. Note, it is a good idea to give an extra margin all round. All important detail must be well within the above areas, as some projectors have peculiar masks and vital parts may not be projected. The size of artwork lettering and detail depends on the size of the projected image and the maximum viewing distance expected.

Further reading 40, 48, 61, 64

12 Language laboratories

These usually contain a number of booths each equipped with a tape recorder and ear phones. The purpose is to give individualised audio-teaching.

In this chapter I am not going to discuss the various types of language laboratory nor their main uses. I hope rather to indicate which visual media might be used and for which purposes.

Description and discussion

Technically any media can be used in the language laboratory. The descrip-tion and discussion section will concern the most suitable form of various media as well as their use in the language laboratory.

The main use of visuals in the language laboratory is largely the same as in the classroom:

— to motivate the students to involve themselves in the language activity,
— to give a believable context for the language activity,
— to help the students to understand the written or spoken text,
— to give non-verbal information which is to be used by the students in manipulative work or in production (oral or written composition),
— to enable the students to show non-verbally that they have under-stood what they have read or heard,
— to help the teachers to explain points to the students.

Visual media in the language laboratory may be used by the student or by the teacher.

Visual media for self instruction are limited by:

a physical convenience — must be manageable in the confines of the booth,

b   need for clarity of use — must be self explanatory. The visual design and layout must be clear and unambiguous,
Examples include: books, workcards, film strips projected on small viewers. Some language laboratories also have video tape displays in each booth. Others have teaching machines for the integration of programmed reading and writing.

Visual media for use by the teacher are limited by:

a   physical convenience — the teacher must be able to operate the apparatus and work from the console; for example the remote control of slide and film strip projector is an advantage,
b   visibility — the visual must be visible from every booth,
c   cleanliness — the medium must be dust and dirt-free or the tapes will be affected; for example, one must use water colour pens on whiteboard rather than chalk on blackboard,
Examples include: whiteboard, magnet board, overhead projector, filmstrip and slide projectors, wall charts, posters and pictures, and occasionally film projectors.

Language laboratories are closely associated with the work of the behaviourist psychologists; the methods used are still largely based on stimulus — response methods and habit formation.

When pictures are used in this, now traditional, method it is in the following way:

a   A text is played on the tape. A sequence of pictures helps the student to get the meaning.
b   The student repeats.
c   The student reproduces the text cued by the pictures.
d   Then several new pictures provide cues for manipulation work i.e. for the substitution of parts of a sentence or for 'filling in' purposes.
e   Pictures are used to cue answers for questions on the tape.
f   Pictures are used to stimulate oral composition.

Leslie Upton (see Further reading 77) suggests that the student is not usually compelled in this method to consider meaning at points c) and d) but has merely to make a correct memory association or mechanical manipulation. He suggests, in order to overcome this merely mechanical response, that the student at point c) move on to a series of questions and that the order in which the pictures are referred to be changed. At this point, therefore, the student has to scan the whole page and select the relevant picture. He thus cannot answer the question without taking account of meaning.
Example:

Recorded question	*Student's response*
Le touriste, où va-t-il?	À la Tour Eiffel.

The student's response is derived from one of several pictures. It is important to note the contribution made by the pictures. Besides giving the student something other than the disembodied voice on which to concentrate, they relieve the burden of memory. He is expected to remember the structures and vocabulary, but not who was going where in each case. Without some such help, it is impossible to give meaning such prominence and so turn the last stage of the drills into a sort of mini-comprehension test.

Leslie Upton's pupil's book, *Talk French* (Further reading 76) contains a great number of pictures for this type of work. My only reservation is that the situational content, i.e. the things dealt with by text and pictures. are not in themselves particularly interesting or significant to the student. We do not really care about the tourist in the picture nor where he goes. There is probably a strong case for activities which do not attempt to grip and fascinate the student all the time. However, there are ways to enliven the student's work in the language laboratory on what is in effect drilling in certain sentence patterns or texts, by the introduction of games, quizzes, puzzles, personality questionnaires, etc.

The language laboratory is of great value in giving listening practice. The discussion and examples in the chapter on listening in the previous section are relevant here.

Further reading 43, 77

Further reading for Part Two 8, 20, 22, 23, 30, 31, 33, 34, 35, 37, 47, 49, 55, 66, 84

PART THREE: The perception of visual materials

Introduction

The information in this section is given to help the teacher to evaluate the visual presentation of the material available to him and, to a lesser degree, to provide some reference for his own manufacture of material.

There are, broadly, two questions to be answered. The first is, 'Will each pupil be able to see the material?' (Clarity). The second is, 'Will the pupil recognise and react to the visual forms he sees in a way relevant to what it is that he should do with it?' (Recognition, Expression).

Clarity

The main test of clarity is for the teacher, with or without the students, to view the material from the likely distance of the furthest student. It is surprising how rarely this is done before materials are bought or used.

Short-sighted students should be identified and brought as near to the visual as possible.

Recognition and expression

If the student can clearly see the visual material, he will get information of two types from the forms he sees.

Firstly, he will get information from a recognition of the *content,* for example the viewer recognises in the picture a man running.

Secondly, he will get information of a different kind from the *expressive* qualities of the form, i.e. the composition, shape, colour, tone, line, texture, movement. For example, the viewer not only recognises that a man is running in the picture, but he feels the sense of running through the expressive qualities of the line.

However reasonable the points in this Part may seem, one thing is worth remembering. Little research has been done into the effect of various types and designs of visual materials and the research results available are often contradictory. It is a field plagued with imponderables and variables, not least of which is the reassuring insistence of the individual on interpreting things in his own way. Each research result represents the careful study of an instance. By 'instance' I mean particular visuals used in particular circumstances by particular people.

It seems extraordinary that anyone should want to make a positive generalisation based on one or two instances, however carefully charted they may be.

Often research is done into the effectiveness of single examples of types of representation, for example, a line drawing and a photograph. Conclusions are then frequently drawn about the comparative effectiveness of these media in general. Yet the examples can in no useful way be said to be representative of the variety of purposes to which such representation may be put.

As an example, let the reader consider all the variety of line drawings in this book. Could any one of them be used in an experiment as an absolutely typical representative of all the others?

In conclusion, I feel that as much research as possible should be done, and read, by all interested parties. However, the uniqueness of each result should be remembered, and only after many instances have been collected should tentative generalisations be made.

The points in this section are based to some degree on research but are in the main based on empirical beliefs.

I Content

For the practical purposes of this book content will be discussed as distinct from shape, colour etc., though obviously those elements are necessary to convey the information we need in order to recognise the content.

The amount of content

Very simple drawings of objects are often not recognised until the artist adds some crucial detail. In simple line drawing crinkly leaves 'make' the tomato, the 'eyes' make the potato and the star and pock marks the orange.

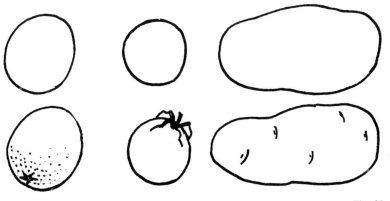

Fig. 68

Connected with the careful selection of information given in a drawing or photograph. is the selection of a position of the object which most satisfactorily presents to us the information we need for recognition. The reader might like to study each phase in the drawings below, noting down the importance of the change of viewpoint which reveals new information, finally making recognition possible. (Cover b,c,d while studying a, etc.).

Fig. 69

a   a view of the saucepan on a level with the eye.
b   a view from above, revealing the characteristic quality of roundness but in this instance a less characteristic view of the handle.
c   a more *characteristic* view of the handle.
d   turned slightly, the joint of handle and pan adds further information which may help us to recognise the saucepan more quickly.

To consider this idea further the reader might consider what is the most characteristic and easily recognisable view of an aeroplane, a house, a person walking and a walking stick.

It is not only in pictures that the adding of crucial information is significant. If the materials producer wants the student to recognise a questionnaire or a language magazine as being like the real thing, then significant detail must be added – the type of paper used, the shape and size of it, the typeface, the layout and column sizes etc.

The relationships between the objects and people depicted will be noticed and recognised by the student if the situation is well chosen and enough visual information provided.

However, the teaching of meaning is only part of our concern in language teaching. Hence making objects and relationships easily recognisable is only one of our concerns in the designing of visuals. We may want to add information over and above that necessary for recognition of the general class of object, and to give it a credible foreign cultural setting and appearance. Or we may want to add elements to the picture which give a humourous touch or to add qualities and information to give a dramatic quality. Every item of visual information given in the visual material by either the publisher or the teacher at the blackboard *can* be chosen to do a particular job– it often isn't.

2 Shape and composition

These two posters are part of a series of 120 designed to be seen from the back of a classroom. They are intended for 9 year old children learning French. The very simple, clearly differentiated shapes are easy to see and distinguish (clarity), the basic shape differences between the two boys makes them easy to recognise and to differentiate, and this also applies when the two boys are depicted on a far smaller scale elsewhere (recognition).

Fig. 70

The background shapes are not arbitrary decorative features but are intended to express some of the character of the two boys (expression).

These three characteristics of clarity, recognition and expression also apply to the element of shape in non-pictorial material.

Consider the following figures

Fig. 71

Fig. 72

The small scale on which these materials are reproduced in this book draws one's attentiqn to their composition and to the overall shapes of the various components. *Clarity* is helped, not merely by the size of detail, for example by the size of the typeface but by the clear diviŝion of the components. *Recognition* implies, in this case, recognition of where to start, which text goes with which picture. Recognition might also mean that the student recognises the shape and the layout and relates it to similar publications from the out-of-classroom world. A well-considered and characterful shape and arrangement may help him to recognise quickly the pages, cards or other materials as he looks for them. *Expression.* The use of shape and composition for expressive purposes in printed matter might seem rather far-fetched. However, compare the examples given above. The magazine has a certain amount of movement: contrasts of shape, line and weight of text and titles. These qualities express something of the excitement and interest one expects from a magazine. Compare them with more extreme designs of magazines, newspapers and advertisements which, to be arresting and stimulating deliberately emphasise irregularities and choose striking angles and shapes. The reader (Fig. 72) illustrated here includes some of the quality of 'striking' design but the main emphasis is on the presentation of the text for easy and continuous extensive reading.

Summary

The information in non-pictorial and pictorial material alike must be clearly visible, it must then be recognisable by the students concerned. Sometimes its qualities can be expressively heightened by the shapes and the composition.

3 Solidity and space

These two features are not visual elements so much as the illusion created by visual elements.

Clarity

As this chapter is dealing with illusion it is not directly concerned with clarity, in the sense of being able to see the marks and colours clearly.

Recognition

Solidity and space may have a lot to do with our recognition of the content of visual representations. By giving an object a quality of solidity and by giving the effect that it is detached from the background, we make it more readily identifiable. The interaction between people and between people and objects inevitably takes place in space and often this space is an important factor in our understanding of what is happening, for example a street scene with a car coming and a child crossing the road.

The illusion of solidity and space in pictures is thus an essential type of information for many purposes.

Expression

Solidity and space can be used dramatically to heighten the quality of the viewer's response. This factor is appropriately used in dramatic presentations of stories on film strip, in film or in books.

The hero's gritted jaw is thrown into relief, the villain speeds off into the distance!

4 Colour

Colour is often used in published language teaching materials. Furthermore it is now easy for the teacher when making his own material to add colour by means of the felt-tipped pens available.

Why use colour?

Teachers have found the following ways of categorising colour useful in making decisions.

Descriptive use of colour

Colour can be information, helping us to recognise something. Thinking back to the tomato, potato and orange, colour would have been another form of information we could have added to aid recognition.

Decorative use of colour

It is probably true that people like to see colour in visual material. This is the reason normally given to justify its use. But people don't agree on what is nice decorative colour. So here we have a quandary. There is no objective basis for a choice of one colour rather than another on purely decorative grounds. It is probably a good idea to discuss it with the students who are to use the material.

Expressive use of colour

This *is* a use of colour but is even more difficult to generalise about than a decorative use of colour. However, it is probably reasonable to say that colour may help to stimulate a particular emotional expression when it is in a context in which other elements are contributing to the same effect. On the whole the language teacher may justifiably neglect this aspect of colour.

Diagrammatic use of colour

This is much more significant to the language teacher. Colour can be used to draw attention to certain parts of a picture or diagram or text. Compare a London Underground map with colour and without it.

Colour is here adding to clarity and more particularly to recognition.

Symbolic use of colour

Colour is symbolically used by language teachers, for example, if a gender form is always picked out in a different colour. It is another language for the student to learn. The teacher must judge if it is worth it for his students.

5 Tone

This is the degree of darkness of a colour.

The use of tone can help clarity, and recognition and can add expression.

Clarity

Tonal differences can make shapes easily discernible, for example, the children stand out clearly because of the differently toned background.

Recognition

Tone may be part of the information of a picture which helps us to recognise an object. For example, the dark tone of a policeman's uniform is a very characteristic feature. The tone of a car is not important for our recognition of it.

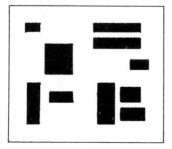 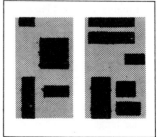

Fig. 73

Expression

This may be controlled as music by the amount and relationship of contrasting or harmonising tones.

Sharp contrasts will tend to attract attention. On the other hand, sharp contrasts all over a picture would send the eye shifting all over the place looking for a main element.

An area of light tone laid evenly over a mass of detail can bring together and make digestible a mass of detailed information. (see Fig. 73)

6 Line

Clarity

Line by itself is not clear for long distance viewing; however, used to emphasise the edge of shapes it is useful, for example in wall posters.

Recognition

Line is probably most useful in making things recognisable, in delineating the bits of information which contribute to our recognition of objects and relationships, the leaves on the tomato, the eyes in the potato, facial expressions, torn pockets, coins, clocks.

Expression

Line also has great potentiality for giving expression. Line can be rather like handwriting; the form the marks take is governed not only by what is being described but by the personality and feelings of the describer.

Unfortunately we cannot count on a consensus of opinion. A thin line may be taken as delicate by one person or feeble by another; a jagged line as being vigorous and positive by one and as self-conscious and shallow by another.

It is safer for the teacher to ask simply: does the line describe the objects clearly and recognisably?

7 Movement

Movement can add to clarity. We might be able to pick out the rabbit when it moves and lose it when it stops. This, however, is not the main function of movement as far as language teaching is concerned. Movement, more importantly, is a type of information which may make certain objects, actions and relationships more recognisable. Of particular importance for language teaching is para-linguistic communication through behaviour, gesture, facial expression, and which can often be conveyed by movement.

In more general terms the addition of movement brings the visual material one step nearer a life-like impression, which may be important for motivation.

However the representation of continuous movement is not always

necessary or desirable. Very often we *want* a still picture to give us time
to study it. If we do want to show a sequence of actions and events, then
very often the main points in that sequence can be shown quite adequately
in a series of still pictures. We have the movement of change represented,
and retain the advantages of the still picture.

Sequences of still pictures are used in film strips, wall posters, overhead
transparencies and by the teacher on prompt cards for guided composition, or prompt cards for guiding dialogue reproduction. Often the essential
aspect of movement is the change from one position to another rather
than actual motion. In this sense a sequence of stills effectively shows

Fig. 74

movement, the intermediate minor changes, not shown, are implied. A self-evident relationship between stills must be kept; the amount of change left out must be gauged according to the learner's age or to how much he knows already.

These 8 frames from a 60 frame picture story on film strip show some of the ways of helping the viewer so to connect the frames that he hardly notices the gaps. I have taken the opportunity of pointing out the expressive use of shape and composition in these pictures.

Frame 47 Sets the scene. The first frame shown here is in fact the first one of a new sequence in the story. The next 6 frames will show events taking place on the road and the following sequence will take place on the beach below.

Frame 48 Connecting links: the moon, the tree, the track. A new viewpoint is taken which makes the action of the heroes as important as the scene. Details from the previous frame are now bigger and more significant. The new viewpoint, on a level with the heroes, makes the viewer empathise with them. In the previous frame we saw them more objectively. Note that the viewpoint or the position of the person who made the picture is shown by the horizon level. This level coincides exactly with the level of the heroes.

Frame 49 There is no moon and no tree to connect us with the previous frame, the road signs are the main connecting link. There is rather a lot of action missing between this frame and the last. The children have run to the barriers and moved one of them.

Frame 50 Again this is a shift of viewpoint. The children act as a connecting link with the previous picture but the artist was careful to include the road signs from the previous frame and the motorbike.

Frame 51 Into this, now recognisable scene, appears the villain. His coming would be expected by pupils from the text and the sound of a car's engine on the tape. Note the viewer's eye level again coincides with that of the heroes.

Frame 52 In this picture the sudden violence of the criminal is shown by the drawing but also expressed by the composition, shapes and lines. Various lines and shapes seem to split the picture in various directions – the car door, the barrier and the criminal's body. The secretive approach of the boy to steal the key is not only shown but expressed by stressing the gap between criminal and boy: a gap which, no doubt, the girl is watching.

Frame 53 Then the criminal turns and sees the boy. The connecting links with the previous picture are there. The line of the hillside helps to emphasise the 'catching sight' Note that the key – a small but central object is given prominence in spite of its size by placing it in the middle, in isolation against a big area empty of features.

Frame 54   Perhaps the reader would like to analyse this frame. Note that this frame is starting a new, though related sequence.

Another sequence of still pictures in this book which might be examined is Fig. 64.

8   Realism to symbolism

I have, in the chapters above, tried to categorise visual elements and to discuss them in a way relevant to some of the activities we want to promote in language teaching. Perhaps there is another way of categorising visual material which might help the teacher to evaluate, to design or to use it. This way of categorising relates to the amount of visual information which is given or needed. Briefly, colour sound movie film can contain a lot of information, a pinman drawn by the teacher cannot give very much information. Two points before this idea is developed: firstly, although each medium or mode has a potential maximum amount of information it might present, it does not follow that it need be used in this way. This is

Fig. 75   Realism

Fig. 76 Realism

Fig. 77   Expressive realism

Fig. 78 Selective realism

important. For example, if pictures with a minimum amount of information are needed it is usually assumed that photography is the wrong medium because it is normally used to show a mass of information. However photography can produce very simple images indeed. It would be quite possible to have a line drawing giving more information than a photograph. Secondly, the theme of this book is that there is no single mode which is right for language teaching.

In most published courses only one or two modes are used, whatever the student is expected to get from or do with the visual material – like the cook who used a frying pan and a high flame for baking bread, preparing soup, omelette, hamburgers, stews, rice pudding and jam tarts: his hamburgers were quite good.

It might help teachers to see a graded list of examples. What sort of activities might each be appropriate for? The most appropriate mode or type of representation should be used whenever possible. Perhaps the reader might look at Figs. 75-83 and decide what each mode could be used for.

Fig. 79   Simplified realism

Fig. 80   Stylisation

Il pleut dehors. . . .

Fig. 81   Cartoon

Fig. 82   Stereotype

Fig. 83
Pictograph

Stylisation (Fig. 80)

This example is only one type of stylised drawing, and of course it is only a personal interpretation which puts it in this category. Stylisation means in this sense the style being more important to the artist and consequently to the viewer than the content. Illustrators often develop a style so that they may become known by it. Publishers reinforce this by then remembering the artists more easily and commissioning them. For decorative purposes such style may be attractive, but it can be seen in the drawings illustrated below that, for conveying information, this emphasis on style is, for most functions, a mistake in language teaching. (Figs. 84-87)

Fig. 84 (top)
Fig. 85 (left)
Fig. 86 (above)

Fig. 87

Style as such, i.e. an artist's characteristic use of visual elements, is not a thing to be condemned, provided the language teaching function is fulfilled.

Symbols (Figs. 88,101)

Symbols are useful and widely used. In a sense the communication itself is based on spoken and written symbols. The question for the language teacher is: should he add to these symbols?

If the symbols are useful and can be introduced a few at a time and are then frequently used, most students will have little difficulty with them.

Symbols can be classified into three types:

Pictographs are, effectively, very simple pictures recognisable by the student. *Concept-related symbols* may remind the student of some quality of the concept. *Arbitrary symbols* bear no relation to the concept symbolised. Clearly the first two types of symbol are the easiest to learn, use and probably to remember.

Michael West in an article in *ELT (ELT XX* No. 3 May 1966 Language Without Words) gave the following symbol sentences containing all three classifications of symbol.

Fig. 88

Advantages of the use of symbols

1 Non-concrete or abstract references can be made without the use of the foreign language or the mother tongue.

    e.g.   starting ↑ going to → in ⊙

This extends the range of help from visuals, normally limited to what can be pictured.

2 Symbols are often quick to do.

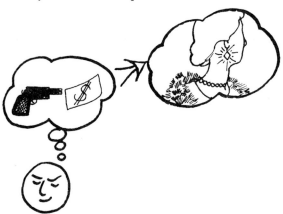

Fig. 89

Disadvantages of the use of symbols

1 It is yet another language to be learnt, interpreted and remembered.
2 If mixed with other conventions, particularly realistic representations, for example, in a presentation filmstrip story, they may detract from the realism of the simulated context.

9 Typefaces and lettering

What a specialist subject this is! Yet the teacher is a major consumer of printed materials, and put end to end, the amount he writes would no doubt stretch round the globe. Below are some ways of evaluating printed or written text and some suggestions which might help the teacher to make materials with text more successful. (More tips on lettering — see How to do it.)

Clarity

Is the text to be seen in a book or on a projected image?

Ability to see the marks clearly depends on the individual's eyesight, on the degree of contrast of the mark with the background, on the size of the mark and the distance of the viewer from it. Certain colour contrasts are said to aid visibility.

Generally, black lettering on white paper or white on black will be the most visible. Some experts strongly recommend white lettering on dark areas for projection. The degree of contrast is also affected by the amount of light available.

The size of the letter is related to the distance away of the furthest pupil. It is usually recommended that black lettering on a white background should be about 2½ cm high to be easily visible at 8-9 metres. Text in books can be virtually any size: it is a matter more of recognition than of clarity.

Recognition

Who is being asked to recognise the text? An early reader or a person not used to the script of the target language will obviously find far more difficulty than a person familiar with the script, who is merely learning to read the target language. However, we can all be affected by problems of recognition. The form of the letters and of the words they make up, the arrangement of the words and lines of text are the key elements to study.

Recognition of type faces in books, etc.

Recognition of letters for adults is not usually a problem. Certainly, the very common design of type called Press Roman is widely acceptable and is rated quite highly in the research which has been done. However, 'readability', as it is called, has a lot to do with familiarity: Press Roman as a style *may* be less easily recognisable in other countries

Univers is a sans serif face.

Press Roman is a serif face.

though they share the same script. Press Roman is a serif script. Amongst the sanserif typefaces, Univers is widely acceptable. Which is better, serif or sanserif lettering? The more sanserif writing we see, the more familiar we are with it and the easier it is to read. For this reason research results date quickly. At the moment designers tend to set long texts in a serif face and to use sanserif typefaces in books, magazines etc., intended for short intensive reading. However, the justification for this lies more perhaps in 'expression' than in readability (see next sub-section).

For young children up to 8 it is usual to insist on a typeface similar to the style of writing they are taught.

a

note the 'a' and 'g'

b A typewriter typeface

c A Stencil Typeface

Fig. 90

Incidentally the letters produced by typewriters and by stencil kits, the main aids of the teacher, are both heavily criticised by typographers! The former is said to be invariably a poor 'face', the latter a characterless face!

It is usually recommended that the size of the letters, the spaces in-between the lines and the length of the lines are slightly greater than found in newspapers: 9pt or 10pt letters with 2pt leading and a 20 em (about 7½ cm) length of line, to put it in technical language. For ease of recognition I do feel that the ascenders and the descenders of letters should not go too near those of the line above or below. We want the eye to go sideways, not be attracted up or down. This is important for adults and even more so for children. The size of the letters for young children should be large but not gross.

The printing of a block of text with straight sides on left and right is normal but not in my opinion necessary. There are even advantages in having a ragged right edge. Space between letters and words can be consistent and words need not be split. The use of the electric typewriter in cheaper publications is making this ragged right-hand side more common.

This is 11 point Univers with 2 point leading between the two lines.

This is 7 point Univers with 2 point leading between the two lines.
The size of the leading is related to the size of the letters. Fig. 91

Plenty of space around the text seems to help our concentration and pleasure in looking at a page.

Capitals or small letters? (upper or lower case?) I do not think anybody would suggest using capitals for a mass of text. The ascenders and descenders of small letters help us to recognise the *word* they are helping to make. The use of capitals in the conventional way at the beginning of sentences, for names etc., is sensible in that it helps understanding.

There is much more dispute about whether or not to use capitals or small letters for titles, signs etc. The advantage of capitals is that the body of each letter is as big as possible whereas in small letters the body of the letter may only be half the size of the total height taken up by the letters.

Expression in typefaces for books, etc.

This is surprisingly important! I have been told by ten year old children that they did not like their reading books because the letters were too big 'It looks like a kid's book'. They were set in 12pt. Older readers may be put off by an unfamiliar type face and layout of the page. This often happens if the book has been designed in a country foreign to the reader.

Designers choose a page size, a type-face and size and a line length partly according to the *impression* they want to make on the reader. They may not be *solely* concerned that he should read the text easily.

Sanserif faces are, on the whole, associated with an 'up-to-date' feeling.

Certain type-faces and layouts are associated with particular publications or with philosophies, or organisations. Computer lettering may be used to imply 'futurism', letter forms from comics to imply that the content is as much fun as the content of a comic.

Clarity, recognition and expression of typefaces to be projected

It is advisable to use a sanserif face for projection and to give plenty of space between the lines. Heavy lettering (bold) and squeezed-up lettering (condensed) tend to fill in and be difficult to read. Lettering produced by stencils is weak and by typewriters very indistinct.

It is attractive and less eye-straining if white lettering is used on a dark colour.

Further reading for Part Three 1, 27, 29, 61, 72, 81, 82

PART FOUR: How to do it

1 How to get good ideas

Ideas are most likely to come to you if you have colleagues to talk things over with. If you offer them four ideas and only get one back it is still a gain! But it is not only a question of exchanging ideas but of developing them. There is also a gain on the practical side in working with a colleague. If materials have to be made, it is usually easy to duplicate what you are both doing separately and then to give each other a copy. You thereby get two lots of material for the making time of one.

Teachers in Britain are increasingly taking part in workshops held either once a week or for intensive periods of one week. These are sometimes small-scale and informal, sometimes organised by the local Teachers Centre or Regional Language Adviser.

Three starting points

1 First of all do your utmost to take other people's ideas, published or unpublished, and to adapt them to your own purposes! There is no point in spending time on unnecessary research, or trial and error. Have no scruples: the majority of ideas you find are, in fact, adaptations of what other people have done. Actual copying of published material can be an infringement of copyright. Details of the laws relating to this can be obtained from the Publishers' Association.

2 Alternatively, you can start from real things which are likely to interest your students (and which you can get hold of) whatever the subject/ content of them is. For example, don't feel restricted to foreign cultural material. Having got the material and ideas see what might arise naturally out of involvement with the materials and what language would be intrinsic to this activity.

   I have personally taken many of my ideas from materials not intended for foreign language teaching. Given that language is a central or an essential part of most studies, then most studies are possible sources of ideas for the language teacher. In this way many of the examples given are derived from materials intended for English as a mother tongue, (Figs. 30, 34) social studies, (Fig. 50) Religious teaching (Fig. 134), and more generally from the new approaches to the teaching of history and geography. Many of our teaching colleagues in other disciplines are developing very interesting approaches to their teaching.

One of these not yet taken up in foreign language teaching is simulation gaming. There must be tremendous possibilities here for more advanced students.

Incidentally, many materials produced for other subject disciplines might be used directly: these may include maps, graphs and photographs. Also note that free or subsidised educational materials are distributed by many firms, including BP, The British Sugar Corporation and Unilever.

Examples – starting point (2)

You think your pupils might be interested in being able to do simple conjuring tricks. Get a book from the library. Choose an effective trick and one in which certain language items are intrinsic, 'look carefully', 'put this. . . .', 'shut this. . . .', 'open this. . . .'.

You know your adult students are very concerned about time lost through strikes. You get recent statistics from the library (Penguin Book on Statistics) and present them by means of graphs or charts for discussion involving numbers and comparisons.

You see in the newspaper a chart comparing the prices of wine, spirits, tobacco etc., charged by various passenger services to the continent. You use this or an adaptation of it for a discussion of the most competitive prices, of which is the best shipping line for whisky-drinkers. The discussion would lead to the expression of likes and dislikes or to which line would be the more geographically convenient.

You have 36 colour slides from your last holiday in the foreign country. You fear that a long description of the culture shown by the slides would bore your students stiff. So you choose a particular theme; for example, you give them a list of car registration codes and their regional origin. The students then identify where the cars in the slides come from and speculate why they have come from other regions. Or you show the slides and pairs or groups of pupils list down the features they feel are like those in their own country and those which are different.

3 Alternatively, you may start with language items and student activities in mind and search for situations, ideas and materials to which the language and activity would be intrinsic.

In giving examples earlier in the book I have tried to make the majority of them of the type the teacher might adopt and adapt with these three starting points in mind. None of them are the 'right' starting points. All of them are in fact well and frequently used by practising teachers. All work based on these points should arrive at the same point i.e. 'intrinsic language' and 'significant' use of it; their origin to the student is irrelevant.

Examples – starting point (3)

How does one find a good situation for the teaching of a new item, in which the language is intrinsic to the situation and the situation significant to the learner?

It would be a joke to claim there was an easy answer to this. However, given that you need to invent and supply your own situation and cannot take it from somewhere else, then:

1 define closely the particular meaning of the new item you are concerned to present or give practice in,
2 decide which of the skills and which of the specific activities in those skills you are concerned to promote,
3 list down all the situations which come to mind in which the teaching items and the specific activity you are concerned with are central. i.e. 'intrinsic language'.
4 tick those which might interest your pupils,
    tick those ticked ones which you feel can be created by you and the students, including getting hold of the materials, designing them and using them in your circumstances.

In practice the detailed precision of 1 and 2 may be relaxed if a situation occurs which promotes useful and complementary practice.

Recently a young German girl stayed in York with my family. She repeatedly muddled the present perfect and the simple past. I looked for a way, relevant to her current interests, by which I could cause these two tenses to be used contrastively. As she was nearing the end of her stay, we took her tourist map of the city and worked out how she might usefully spend her remaining time. I asked which places she had been to, seen, visited etc. and when or how many times. We used the map to act as a memory cue and to help disguise from her that as far as I was concerned it was an intense bit of contrastive practice in the use of the two tenses.

Taking the same structure, an evening class of housewives might be interested in carrying out a survey on the use of certain shops in their town. Working in pairs, students would establish with each other the number of visits per shop according to a questionnaire. 'Have you been to. . . .', 'How many times have you been there during the last month. . . ', 'When did you last go there. . . .', 'What did you spend. . . .'. A class of schoolchildren might do a survey on the popularity of television programmes.

Categories of situation

Another possible help to the teacher might be to look in the list for categories of useful situations.

| Games | By this is meant the fun, competition games played at parties or on radio or television. Games often make repeated use of one or two structures. |
| Humour | Jokes are extremely useful for making language memorable. Caption jokes to drawings are one of the few cases in which |

single isolated sentences are natural.

Physical activities Making things, including models, gadgets or following recipes; also experimenting, including simple science experiments, growing plants; keeping pets; doing things including conjuring tricks. On the whole this is for younger pupils, but may provide an occasional source of welcome change to older students.

Topics Topics of concern to the students and which they will be glad to study in order to solve their problems or satisfy their interests, for example, make-up tips; how to eat well and stay thin; hobbies and fortune-telling; inventions.

Studies A little bit like topics, but with the emphasis on action; for example, the use of questionnaires to carry out social surveys or psychological studies. Alternatively, the study of the occurrence of foreign language words in the local district in names of streets, shops, goods for sale and in the local museum and why they should occur.

Discussions Subjects are chosen likely to promote differences of opinion. Materials such as photographs, charts, graphs etc. can be used as discussion points.

Simulations The general idea is to provide information which may be textual, pictorial, diagrammatic or audial and which together is the raw material of a situation. Students take on the role of participants in the situation. They do not merely learn a dialogue but study the information as given to them and then behave according to their role. The outcome is not predictable but would generally involve all the skills, particularly the productive ones of speaking and the undirected and directed intensive skills of listening and readding. (see Tansey, Further reading 74)

Survivals More controlled simulations based on the situations a foreign visitor/traveller might be in; finding the way, being ill etc.

Journalism *An approach to the devising of materials*
Our most unwilling students read newspapers or look at magazines and comics or watch television and films. Is it *only* the subject which is different? Or is it partly the form? The tabloid papers and popular television do take some subjects which are, in normal circumstances, beyond the interest of the mass of people and make them interesting and relevant. Our keenest students and the majority, no doubt, of teachers watch, listen to and read things not strictly academic. What is the attraction? Is there anything we can use to make our materials more enjoyable?

Many exercises are headed, 'Answer these questions'. Yet, depending on the nature of the questions, one might have headed them, 'Have you got a good memory? Answer these questions and find out', or 'What do you know?' or 'Are you a born detective?', or 'Are you honest?' or 'Do you *really* like your friend?' The alternative headings intrigue the reader; he wants to follow them up.

Below are a few tips on intrigue and follow-up!

Basically, it is a matter of spotting an interest or a need of the student or creating one. The media the pupil is interested in in out-of-classroom life will indicate to you how these subjects might best be presented. Surprise, the unexpected, is an obvious standby. One of my own best lessons was based on having hidden a variety of vegetables in my clothes and all over the room. I produced the first one, in apparent astonishment, half way through the lesson.

Logic is useful for analysis but does not necessarily guide one to intriguing communication. It is often not a successful technique to go from first principles to examples, to go from a to b to c. One can go from the examples to the generalisation, from the problem to the solution from the controversial statement to the discussion. Alistair Cooke in his 'Letter from America' very often begins his talk on the BBC with a detailed account of an incident without giving any hint of general statement. The incident is comprehensible to us, we can identify with it, we attend.

Contrast is another old standby. How many articles begin, 'Britain is a land of contrasts?' Any country or subject can be treated in this way. The contrast of features is good because the receiver contributes by his effort to see the relationship. Making the receiver contribute is one of the secrets of communication. The poor and the rich are shown, the weak and the strong, the loud and the soft, the rough and the smooth. The principle of contrast applies to the content and to the form. Visually a large photograph can be interestingly offset by several small photographs, a colour production by several black and whites.

Sources of pictures

Advertisement leaflets for cars, household goods, paint manufacturers catalogues, clothes, holidays.

Propaganda leaflets for road safety, the country code.

Personal old Christmas Cards, calendar pictures.

Pictorial 'literature' comics, magazines, games, playing cards.

Industrial Educational Material Many firms have an educational service and supply materials free or very cheaply. They are often very good.

See also Appendices 2 and 3

Further reading 5, 15, 26, 36, 42, 54, 57

2 What you need to make visual materials

No materials for particular media are listed. See specialist literature.

Basic kit for teacher

H.B. pencil
4 nylon tipped colour pens
4 broad felt-tipped markers
1 2cm decorator's brush
1 craft knife (scalpel variety)
1 50 cm metal or perspex ruler
1 pair of scissors
1 pencil sharpener
1 set square
1 stapler
1 pair of compasses
4 big bulldog clips

For lettering:
1 5 cm alphabet stencil
1 2 cm alphabet stencil
1 stencil brush size 3
1 reservoir pen (for stencils)

Extras
Pantograph
Rubber stamps of letters, numbers, objects
Templates of letters, numbers, objects

Kit for workshop

Long arm stapler
Stapling gun
Hole punch
Eye punch
Edge binder
Guillotine
plus all basic kit of teacher

Extras
Spirit Duplicator
Ink Duplicator
Offset Lithographic Printing Machine
Silk screen printing equipment
Photocopying machine

Roneo Lateral Filing ⎫
Railex Filing   ⎬ Classroom Display Matter
Lightbox for tracing and slide viewing
35 mm camera + arc lights
Photographic enlarger
Typewriter with big size type face

Basic consumables

Paper (60lbs is a reasonable quality)
Cartridge paper — (adaptable)
Newsprint — (cheap, tears easily, thin)
Sugar paper — (absorbent, often coloured)
Card   (3 sheet card is thin. 12 sheet card is thick.)
Manilla card available in colour
Mounting card

Adhesives

Petroleum based gum for paper (no wrinkling)
Office paste for paper (cheap)
PVA or Copydex for other materials
(Up-to-date advice best sought from local supplier.)

Adhesive tape

Double-sided adhesive tape

Inks

Indian Ink — small bottle
White Ink — small bottle

Protective materials

Self adhesive transparent film
Transparent plastic envelopes
(Up-to-date advice best sought from local supplier.)

Other

Drawing pins. Split pins. Paper clips.
BLU-TACK by Bostik Ltd.

The yearbook of the magazine *Visual Education* includes an excellent up-to-date and summarised list of equipment and materials available, including pens, drawing aids, stencils, inks, paints, chalk and crayons, letters, flannelgraphs, plastic display boards, paper, adhesives, protectives, magnet boards. Also sources of free or subsidised educational publications. Also an extensive bibliography of books on audio-visual media in education.

3 Tips-drawing and lettering

I have tried to give in this section enough suggestions for the language teacher to be able to design and make materials. If the teacher becomes very interested in materials preparation, then he will need more detail and should consult the many books concerned with techniques. (see Further reading 7, 20, 33, 62, 63.)

Tracing

Method 1 If the paper you want to use is thin then you may be able to see the image to be copied through it. If you can't, then place both the paper with the image on it and the paper to be traced on against the window, preferably with strong sunlight behind. This is the fastest way of tracing.

Alternatively, if you are working at night, put a table lamp on the floor and rest the picture and the paper on a sheet of glass placed above the lamp.

Method 2 Use tracing paper. Trace the picture. Scribble a soft pencil on the back of the tracing paper. Put the tracing paper down on the area to receive the tracing and draw on top of the tracing.

Enlarging

Method 1 Divide the picture to be copied into squares. Divide the paper you are going to transfer it to into squares. Copy from one square on the picture to a similarly positioned square on the new paper. If the squares on the new paper are twice as big as those on the picture, then the enlargement will be twice as big. The same technique can be used to copy or to reduce a picture. It was a technique used by Renaissance painters!

Method 2 Enlarge the picture by epidiascope, or other projector, throwing the image on to the paper you want to use for the copy.

Method 3 Use a pantograph in the way described by the maker. This is a fairly cheap (75p approx.) instrument and quite useful.

These three enlargement techniques produce an accurately proportioned picture. However, don't be disappointed by the detail. That will appear wobbly. It is quite usual to have to go over the line work with more precision.

Pinmen

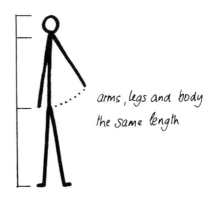

arms, legs and body
the same length

Fig. 92

The basic pinman

For the sake of speed and the minimising of distracting elements the pinman need have no other features, for example, hands, shoulders, hips, neck. Exceptions to this guiding rule are referred to under 'Boxmen', page 122.

All lines for the arms, body and legs should be equal in length. This is a very simple principle, worth remembering. Elbows and knees should be half way along their respective limbs.

The lines should be straight in most cases. They should also be bold not sketchy. If the pinmen are to be viewed the length of a classroom the lines should be thick. The lines should meet the body line rather than stop short: many little gaps add confusion.

Badly drawn pinmen

Fig. 93

a Hips take time to draw and may lead to odd effects as in this drawing.
b The proportions are rather odd. The hips are too wide. The hands are disproportionate and do not reflect the character of hands.
c The neck is ugly, the body too short, the head too big. The thickness of the line is ugly.
d The neck is ugly. The line is crude. The hands are pathetic.
e The lines are feeble, the gaps disturbing, the hands distracting.

The walking and running pinman

Fig. 94

Very slow walking is shown by drawing the arms and legs very near to the vertical. Faster movement is shown by opening the arms and legs out. Some teachers do not know which way to bend the legs and arms. The guiding rule is always to make the legs bend forwards and the arms backwards. Note the fine distinctions which can be made between running quickly and sprinting.

Does your pinman fall over?

Fig. 95

The pinman should not look as if it is falling over unless that is the intention. The principle we all learned at about the age of one year is applicable to pinmen. The centre of gravity of the body, roughly the abdomen, should be over the supporting point or between the supporting points or between the supporting points and the ground. Compare the drawings below. Which pinmen will fall down? Can you say why? Try standing like the ones you think will fall down. What do you do to stop yourself falling?

Draw a vertical line through the centre of gravity of the body. Mark the point nearest to this line which is supporting the body. This should indicate why some of the pinmen appear to be overbalancing while others appear to be balanced.

Copy the drawings below and add the missing legs in such a position that the pinmen will not fall down.

Fig. 96

Looking

Sometimes the teacher may wish to show that the pinman is looking in a certain direction. This is easy to achieve; simply add a nose.

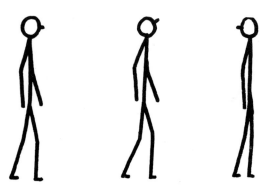

Fig. 97

Fig. 98   The pinman in action

Pinmen with characters

To distinguish between characters or between a man and a woman add a characteristic tag. Only add tags if there is a practical reason. It takes time. It can be distracting if it is not essential to the message. Overused tags will come to lose impact.

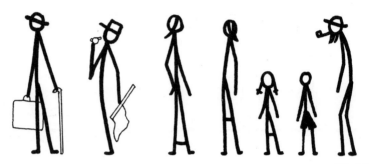

Fig. 99

Boxmen

There is usually not enough time to use more than lines when drawing on the blackboard. However, the teacher may want to draw 'proper' figures on workcards, flashcards, wall charts or when making flannelgraph figurines. These solid figures add interest, give character and increase clarity when seen over a long distance.

If a very simple principle is followed without change nobody need fail!

1 Draw a box for the body, thin seen from the side, wide seen from the front.
2 Draw the head.
3 Draw each of the four limbs to the corners of the box exactly like a pinman.
4 When 3 is satisfactory draw the *inside* of the legs and arms copying the outside lines exactly.
5 Draw circles for the hands and triangles for the feet.

Fig. 100   How to build a boxman

If at any point greater naturalism is attempted it will look wrong unless drawn by someone with a natural drawing talent.

Note, bare legs and arms are usually quite clear if left as single strong lines. Any attempt to indicate shape to legs and arms is likely to look dreadful.

Symbols

Symbols can be very useful if they are understood, this is usually just a question of familiarity with them. Many more examples can be found in comic strip drawing and cartoon.

Fig. 101

Faces

The face can be any shape and time should not be spent on trying to make a 'correct' shape. An easy guide to the position of the features is to place the eyes one third of the way down the face and the bottom of the nose two thirds of the way down. A baby's features appear to be much lower on the face.

Fig. 102

Noses, like those in the drawings above, are easy to do and look three-dimensional enough to blow!

Expressions are shown by the mouth and eyebrows. It is helpful to draw the eyes and nose first and to add the eyebrows and mouth afterwards.

Fig. 103

The expressions are not unambiguous though one may achieve a wide consensus of opinion. They tend to be no more and no less unambiguous than expressions on real faces. These few lines are, in fact, not symbols in the full sense but abbreviations and exaggerations of what we know. Real faces, photographs and artists' drawings could be examined and copied with this in mind. The teacher can soon gain control of basic types of expression but he must actually draw them and keep on chopping and changing until it comes right. Pinmen and pinfaces, easy though they are, do need *some* perseverance in the actual making of them: boring journeys, tedious lectures, fag ends of days are ideal if your spirit isn't too crushed.

Note the individual features change shape; eyebrows straighten, curve or become angular. However, equally important is that they change position on the face and in relation to each other; anger tends to bring the features near together; unconcern tends to distance them.

If you are having difficulty in drawing an expression, find something to copy, either a photograph or your own acting in a mirror — this is what professional illustrators often do.

Fig. 104

Tags can be added to distinguish characters.

Animals or objects

I can give below a number of drawings to copy but what suggestion can be given to the teacher to help him draw other objects? It's not easy. It would be silly to pretend that it is. However, there are two starting points which might be useful.

1 What is the basic shape (or combination of shapes) of the object? That is the first information one needs for recognition.
2 What little characteristic do you associate with it? This *must* follow the answer to question 1.

Side view or front view?

Choose whichever view will show the most characteristic features of the

Fig. 105

object or action you wish to represent. Side views are probably the best for chairs, cars, animals and for most actions because one can show the movement of limbs and imply that the object is going across the page. Front views show the characteristics of television sets, houses, standing people. A view of the top and the side or front, helps to show the volume of an object; this is important in the case of a cup or an open suitcase. (Fig. 69)

Further reading 50, 85, 86

Distance and space

Normally make your drawings go across the paper. Distance into the picture from front to back is usually not essential and is an extra bother to do satisfactorily. With these 'straight across' pictures don't give, by accident, a cue to depth! For example it's a good idea to keep the figures or objects along a base line. Things standing above this will appear to be further away.

How can one give an impression that there is space in the picture and that objects have a certain place in that space? It should be remembered, of course, that visual cues do not give rise to the same interpretation all over the world.

Fig. 106

Overlap One of the easiest ways is to overlap the object you want in the foreground across part of the object supposed to be in the background.

Up and down Objects which stand on the ground will usually have their base line low in the picture if near and high if far away.

Size If the drawing appears to be fairly realistic we have an expectancy of size relationships. Thus, if a house appears smaller than a man, we assume it must be far away. However, this is a convention easily and acceptably broken.

Light and dark   Although in life and in pictures there is no exclusive association between distance from the spectator and the light or dark tone of objects, it is possible, particularly in line drawing, to imply that an object is far away by drawing it lightly and near to by drawing it more boldly.

Perspective   Some simple ideas might be useful. The first is based on the eye level of the person who drew or photographed the scene. If you stand on a railway line the level is where the rails appear to meet. If the landscape is flat the horizontal lines and edges of many symmetrical objects will appear to drop or to rise to this level.

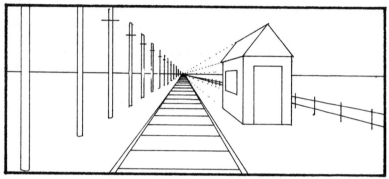

Fig. 107

Many of the lines will meet at the same point on this eye level. Others will meet at a different point on the eye level.

This is only the first step in perspective drawing. It is probably all that is necessary for the language teacher.

Further reading 50, 85, 86

Lettering   (see also Perception, Typefaces)
The teacher will want to write texts and titles on the blackboard, workcards, wall charts, transparencies for the overhead projector. He is more likely to handwrite these texts but he may sometimes use a typewriter.

Typewriters

The teacher can either try to type on the actual visual material or he can paste down his typewritten sheet in position, for example, on the wallchart. The advantage is reasonable legibility and orderliness. The disadvantage is that typewritten texts are not legible from very far away and do not produce a big enough letter for legibility on overhead projector transparencies. Typewriters can be bought with a big size of letter suitable for use on transparencies and better for workcards and wallcharts (group-use wallcharts).

(For information concerning typewriters with large typefaces contact: OEM Reprographic Ltd., 140-154 Borough High St, London SE1.)

Handwriting

In all cases the text must be legible. Two major contributions to legibility are the clarity of individual letter forms and the distinctive shape of groups of letters in certain words. Capitals do not give a distinctive shape to a word.

Compare **SHAPE** and shape

The recommendation for handwriting is a semi printed formation of letters.

It is recommended that hand-writing be based on a semi-printed formation of letters 
Fig. 108

More tips on handwriting

Keep your lettering on a horizontal line (usually rubbed out afterwards!).
Keep the letters open and clear.
Keep the letters fairly close together.
Keep the upper and lower strokes fairly short.
Keep at least two letters' body height between lines.
Keep the left-hand edge vertical.

Broad-tipped felt pens are an important innovation of recent years. They enable the teacher to produce strong colourful lettering at speed and without mess. Special lettering pens are rather difficult to use.

Titles and sub-titles

These can be handwritten, cut out, done with the aid of a stencil or by tracing newsprint.

Capitals or a combination can be used. The same tips given above apply.

Handwritten titles

These will look amateurish if you copy a formal printed style. Fancy styles are easy to do, fast, characterful, eye-catching and hide incompetence!

Fig. 109

Keep the holes as small as possible. Keep the base line horizontal.

Double pen lettering

Fasten two pens or pencils together. Always hold them at one consistent angle.

Cut-out letters

A surprisingly successful although slightly more time-consuming technique is to cut out letters with a craft knife from coloured papers. The letters are then stuck down. These letters should be no more than sketched out. Their patently varying character, but with sharp sides and angles, is the secret of their attraction and apparent professionalism.

Fig. 110

Newsprint lettering

The headline letters of newspapers can either be traced or cut out.

Stencils

Stencils can be bought for a variety of letter types and sizes. Either a pen is used to make 'line' letters or a brush is stamped on, making 'area' letters.

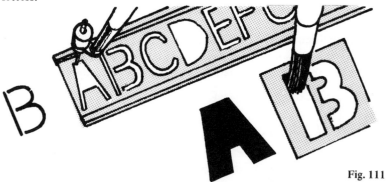

Fig. 111

Planning titles — space

The easiest way is to start the title on the left and to go on until it finishes.

If it must be central, then you can either print it on a separate piece of paper and paste it in position or find the middle of the title and start there, working outwards.

Further reading 3, 41, 63, 64, 72

Cutting out

The craft knife is essential for all teachers who intend making their own materials. It saves time, makes less mess, and is incomparably more flexible than a pair of scissors.

Cutting out of magazines

Put a piece of thin card under the page. Using the point of the craft blade follow the shape you want. The picture will then drop out clean as a whistle. A sharp blade will not drag and tear the paper. You can have a sharp blade by sharpening the one you've got on a carborundum or by buying new ones every few months for a few pennies. This method provides the easiest, quickest and most impressive type of homemade teacher material. For example see Fig. 33.

Cutting card

The craft knife will cut through very thick card. The secret is not to try to cut it at one go but to repeat many light strokes.

Rulers

Metal rulers are particularly good for tearing straight edges.

Scissors

Scissors are essential if children are helping. Craft knives are rather dangerous.

Adhesives

The world of adhesives is in a state of change. Principally one is concerned with adhesives which leave no mess or stain and do not wrinkle paper. The glue used by most studios for paper in this country is petroleum based.

Further reading 14

Protecting your materials

Basically the modern transparent materials are either self-sticking or not, depending on price. The self-sticking types stick like leeches and give the impression of having a wilful life of their own. They reach up and stick to the wrong part of your workcard, to your sleeve, to the table and worse still to themselves. Two ways to deal with this living being:-

a lay down the plastic sticky side up and drop the workcard on to it. Fine for small things.

b lay down the workcard image side up. Fold the plastic round like a magazine. Lower the middle of it on to the middle of the image. Put your hand or a ruler inside and slowly work it out to the outside. Leave enough border to tuck round the back.

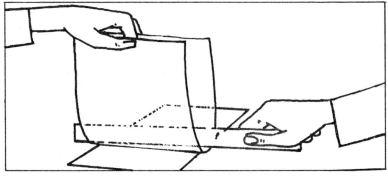

Fig. 112

Non-sticky plastics, cellophanes, etc. can be taped onto the back of the workcard etc.

Cellophane or plastic envelopes are very useful and can be used again and again.

Further reading 11, 14

4 Tips-design and layout

Compare these pairs of designs. What are the differences? In 1b and 2b the text and pictures are placed more symmetrically than in 1a and 2a; in particular the left hand edges lie vertically in relation to each other. Also the bits that are floating about are stabilised and linked by the enclosing rectangle (Fig. 1b) or in the case of Fig. 2b the boring consistency of the rectangles is enriched by the cutting out of the main image from the picture to reveal a more interesting outline.

A regularity and symmetry of design is usually adopted by designers of books and often of wallcharts. They base the design of their pages on a grid which is constant for the entire publication.

The multi-column grids are chosen when there is a variety of material, textual and pictorial. The vertical regularity is probably the most emphasised feature particularly the left hand edge of the columns. However this verticality and horizontality can be broken without losing the harmonising influence of the grid by crossing columns with titles and photographs, usually filling up two columns. This is often done in newspapers, giving them an informal quality, although the basic symmetry remains and prevents one feeling that the page will be difficult to read. (See Fig. 113)

It would probably be advisable for the language teacher to base everything he does on one or other of these grids. Wondering whether

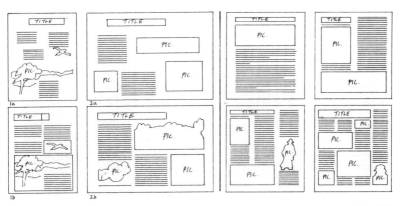

Fig. 113

to use an assymetrical design takes time and the risk of it being weak is quite high. If the teacher does want to have an asymmetrical design, then it is probably a good idea to look through advertisements etc. until an appropriate design is found.

Other design tips which may be useful:

Lettering
In addition to the other suggestions on lettering it is usually advisable not to vary the type and size of the lettering too much on any one piece of material. Perhaps have one type of letter for the main title, one for the sub-titles and one for the rest.

Photographs
They need not always be placed centrally but could on occasion be placed to one side, or go off the edge altogether. They need not always be square but with the craft knife can easily be cut out to reveal an interesting shape.

Fig. 114

Background colours
These need not always be white. Coloured card is easy to come by.

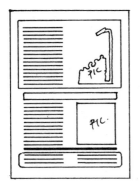  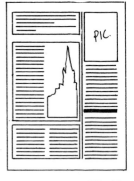

Fig. 115

Line 'Boxes'

Designers often use rectangles or 'boxes' to collect together information meant to be seen together or to reduce a raggedy appearance. Boxes can be square-cornered or round cornered. Boxes can be patches of different coloured or toned paper. See Fig. 115.

Lines

Lines can be used like boxes to give an appearance of order or to separate off certain parts.

Big and small

Very big photographs can be set against a few little ones. Very big titles combined with fine lettering all make for richness of contrast.

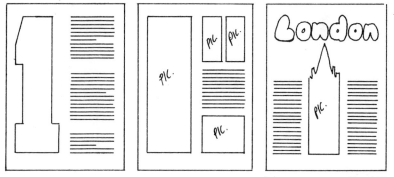

Fig. 116

Thin and thick

It is often visually enriching and also less confusing if one type of visual element is drawn in a light line, another in a heavy line. This simple idea sounds fussy but it can make the world of difference to many uninspiring, if neat, visuals.

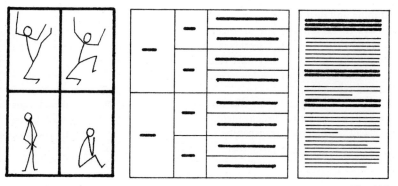

Fig. 117

Space

Don't feel that every bit of paper should be covered. Many effective designs include empty spaces. One good reason is that people don't think they will have to make an extraordinary effort to get through a mass of information!

Amount of information

In order to present a not overpowering amount of information it is often better to make two or more visuals.

Reading direction

Most scripts are read from right to left and top to bottom. This is the usual way to order information on workcards and charts. Division into columns particularly with dividing lines will, of course, guide the eye *down* the columns.

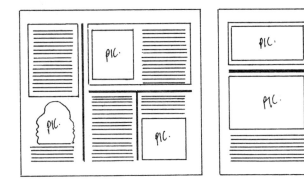

Fig. 118

Have a look at a newspaper or magazine to see how the designer has guided your attention and how he has 'collected' sections together.

Planning and designing

It pays to sketch out the arrangements you think might be satisfactory. It takes little time and avoids spoiling valuable material. Many of the illustrations in this chapter were done in this way.

General relevance

Most of the suggestions in this chapter apply to all the visual materials teachers are likely to design, including workcards, worksheets, wallcharts, overhead projector transparencies and display or bulletin boards.

5 Tips - displaying and manufacturing

Displaying pictures

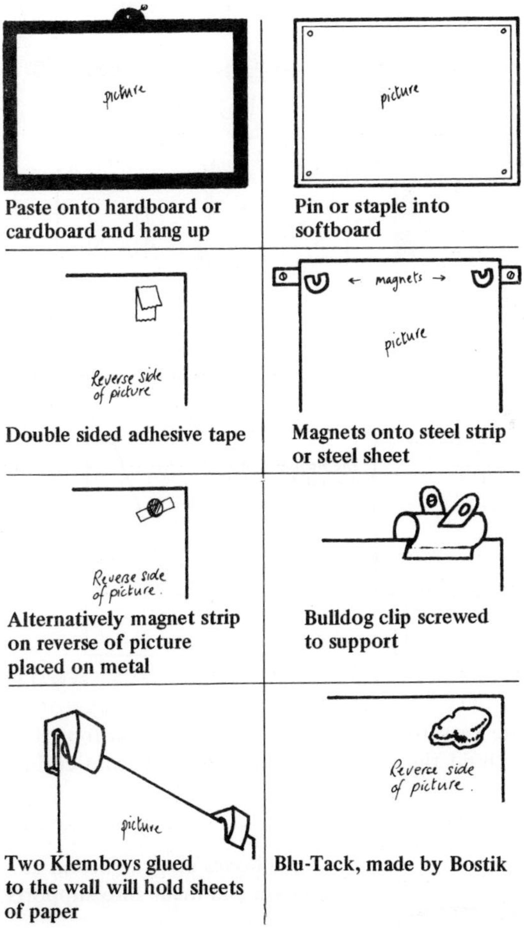
picture
Paste onto hardboard or cardboard and hang up
picture
Pin or staple into softboard
Reverse side of picture
Double sided adhesive tape
← magnets →
picture
Magnets onto steel strip or steel sheet
Reverse side of picture.
Alternatively magnet strip on reverse of picture placed on metal
Bulldog clip screwed to support
picture
Two Klemboys glued to the wall will hold sheets of paper
Reverse side of picture.
Blu-Tack, made by Bostik

Fig. 119

Blu-Tack is one of several products which looks like plasticine and sticks cards to walls etc. It can be detached easily and without spoiling either surface.

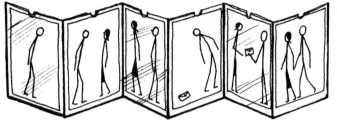

Fig. 120

Clear plastic envelopes can be hinged together. Cards of drawings or words can be put in for guided production or oral/dialogue reproduction etc.

Fig. 121

Wire or string can be stretched between screws. Bulldog clips give permanant display or easy release.

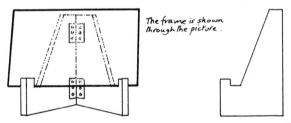

The frame is shown through the picture.

Fig. 122

Portable display boards are easy to make out of stout card, hardboard or wood. A piece of card behind the picture would prevent it from curling over.

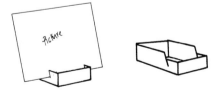

Shoe boxes etc. can be cut as shown and made into supports.

Fig. 123

Magnet boards

Any sheet of template or galvanised iron will make a magnet board. The metal should be glued or screwed to a support surface — hardboard, wood, the wall. The metal can be painted with chalkboard paint or a matt paint.

FRONT   BACK

Fig. 124

This is one way of making a portable magnet board. (Fig. 125)

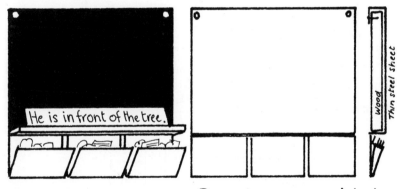

Metal side.
Ledge for sentence card.
Pouches for figurines.

Board side is painted
white for projection.

Fig. 125

Flannel board

Any metal, card or wood support can be covered with flannelette, Dorset crepe, winceyette or old blanket. This can be fixed by glueing or stapling, or hung freely. The support must lean backwards or the figurines will drop off.

The figurines must have flannel material on the back, or surgical lint, sandpaper, Dorset crepe or roughened blotting paper.

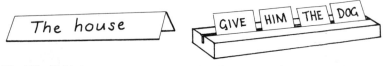

Fig. 126   Folded paper   **Fig. 127   Grooved wooden support**

Further reading 10, 56

Word card displays   (Flexible order)

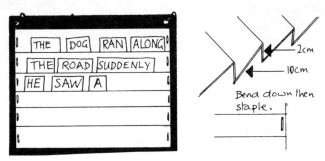

Fig. 128

A large sheet of paper is folded as shown, stapled onto a card or hardboard support.

Word displays   (Inflexible order)

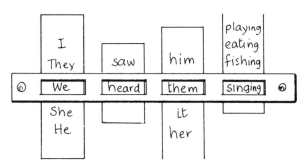

Fig. 129

The main band should be made of stout card. If it is small it can be hand held, if large must be hung on the wall. Leave enough card at either end to press on to give firmness when moving the strips. The windows should be bigger than the strips. The ends of the strips should either have long blanks on them or be folded over, or they will become infuriatingly unslotted.

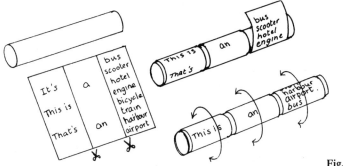

Fig. 130

Take one cardboard roll. Wrap a sheet of paper around it and mark off the circumference. Write the words in columns which will go to make up the parts of sentences. Cut the columns into strips, wrap these around the roll and join the ends with adhesive tape. They should revolve easily.

Wheels

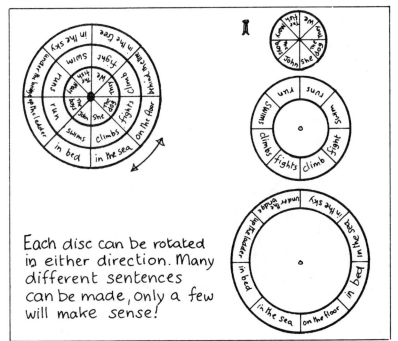

Each disc can be rotated in either direction. Many different sentences can be made, only a few will make sense!

Fig. 131

On each segment of each of the three discs is a part of a sentence. The discs are rotated until the patterns make semantic sense. The discs can be

of cards of different colours if the teacher would like to stress the category
of the component.

(Alternative: use trick question on one segment — joke answer to it on
the other.)

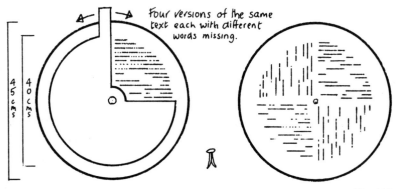

Fig. 132

The same text is repeated in the four segments on the lower card.
However, there are different words missing in each segment. The student
must read intensively, remember and try to establish the completed text.
(This could be quite an extensive text.)

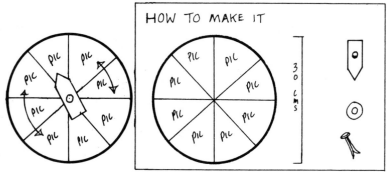

Fig. 133

This wheel is commonly used to cue subject, verb and object for
manipulation practice. The upper card is spun round by means of the
pointer.

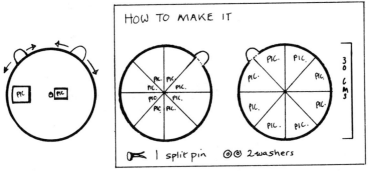

Fig. 134

The window wheel for words and/or pictures.

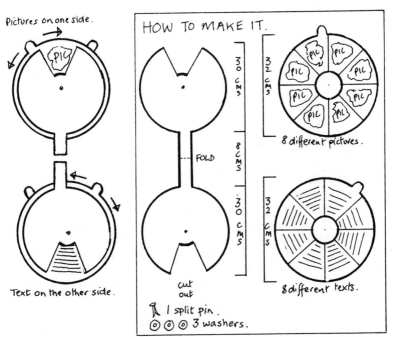

Fig. 135

This device shows pictures on one side and text on the other. It could be used by pupils working in pairs.

Further reading for Part Four 9, 10, 12, 13, 20, 24, 28, 33, 35, 36, 48, 53, 62, 64, 68, 71, 75, 82, 86, 87

Further reading

Please note that some of the books listed below are referred to by number under the Further reading sections following many of the chapters or sections of chapters. For an annotated bibliography of over 700 books on language teaching, readers are referred to *A Language Teaching Bibliography* compiled by the Centre for Information on Language Teaching and the English Teaching Information Centre.

1   ARNHEIM, R. *Art and Visual Perception,* Faber, 1954.
2   BENNETT W.A. 'The Organisation and Function of Visual Material in Second Language Teaching', in *Visual Education,* Feb. 1970.
3   BERRY, JOHNSON AND JASPERT, *The Encyclopaedia of Type Faces,* Blandford.
4   BILLOWS, F.L. *The Techniques of Language Teaching,* Longman, 1965.
5   BOOTHMAN, D.B. et al. *Topical Research Workbooks,* (6 books in the series), Longman, 1969.
6   BRIGHT, J.A. and McGREGOR, G.P. *Teaching English as a Second Language,* Longman 1970.
    BRITISH COUNCIL, A-V Department, Education and Science Division:
7   *Aids to Drawing and Enlarging.*
8   *Audio-visual Material for English Teaching.*
9   *Designing, Making and Assessing Wallcharts and Posters.*
10 *Flannelgraph, Magnetic Board and Plastigraph as Aids to Teaching & Training.*
11 *Information on Materials for Making and Protecting Wallcharts and Handouts.*
12 *Silkscreen Techniques and Sources of Supply.*
13 *Types, Uses and Sources of Duplicators.*
14 *Wet Mounting of Charts, Posters and Pictures.*
15 BUCKBY, M. and GRANT, D. *Faites Vos Jeux.* Materials Development Unit, Language Teaching Centre, University of York.
16 BULL, W.E. *A Visual Grammar of Spanish,* 2nd edition, University of California, 1966.
17 BYRNE, D. and WRIGHT, A. *What Do You Think?* Books 1 and 2, Longman, 1975.
18 BYRNE, D. *Progressive Picture Composition,* Longman, 1966.

19   BYRNE, D. and HALL, D. *Wall Pictures for Language Practice,* Longman, 1974.
20   CABLE, R. *Audio-Visual Handbook,* University of London Press, 1970.
21   *Catalogue of Wallcharts,* Educational Foundation for Visual Aids.
22   *Catalogue of 16 mm films for the foreign language teacher,* Nuffield Foreign Language Teaching Materials Project, Micklegate House, York.
23   *A Classified Guide to Sources of Educational Film Material,* Educational Foundation for Visual Aids and National Committee for Audio-Visual Aids in Education, 1968.
24   CLEMENCE, W. *The Beginner's Book of Screen Process Printing,* Blandford Press.
25   COLE, L.R. 'The Visual Element and the Problem of Meaning in Language Learning', in *Audio-Visual Language Journal,* Vol. IV2 winter 1966/67.
      'The Psychology of Language Learning and A-V Techniques', in *Modern Languages,* Vol XLIX, No. 4, 1968.
26   CONNEXIONS, Penguin Education, Penguin Books, London, (a series of pupils' books.)
27   COPPEN, H. *A Survey of British Research in Audio-Visual Aids, N.C.A.V.A.E.*
28   COPPEN, H. *Wall Sheets: Their Design, Production and Use,* Educational Foundation for Visual Aids.
29   COPPEN, H. *Visual Perception,* Commonwealth Secretariat, Marlborough House, London S.W.1. 1970.
30   CORDER, S.P. *English Language Teaching and Television,* Longman, 1960.
31   CORDER, S.P. *Modern Foreign Language Teaching by Television,* Chap 13 pps 235-251 of Albert Valdman – *Trends in Language Teaching* McGraw-Hill, 1966.
32   CORDER, S.P. *The Visual Element in Language Teaching,* Longman 1965.
33   DALE, E. *Audio-Visual Methods in Teaching,* Holt, Rinehart, Winston.
34   DAVIS, D. *The Grammar of Television Production,* Barrie & Rockliff, 1960.
35   DEVEREUX, E.J.P. *An Introduction to Visual Aids,* The Visual Aids Centre.
36   DOAN, E.L. *Make-it-yourself Visual Aids Encyclopaedia,* G/L Publications, Glendale, California, 1967.
37   *Equipment & Information Departments of the Educational Foundation for Visual Aids,* Price List 1971. EFVA Inf. Dept.
38   FLEMING,G. 'Meaning , Meaningfulness and Association in the Context of Language Teaching Media', in *PRAXIS,* No. 2, 1966, Dortmund Germany.

39   FLEMING, G. SPALENY, E. PEPERNICK, J. *The Didactic Organi-sation of Pictorial Reality in the New Language Teaching Media, PRAXIS* April 1967.

40   FRANCOMBE, A. *Notes on Photo-Play,* pamphlet by Kodak Ltd, London.

41   GILL, E. *An Essay on Typography,* J.M. Dent & Sons, 1960.

42   *Group Work in Modern Languages,* Materials Development Unit, Language Teaching Centre, University of York.

43   HAYES, A.S. *Language Laboratories Facilities,* Oxford University Press.

44   HEATH, R.B. *Impact Assignments in English,* Longman, 1968.

45   HEATON, J.B. *Practice Through Pictures,* Longman, 1971.

46   HEATON, J.B. *Composition Through Pictures,* Longman, 1966.

47   HICKEL, R. *Modern Language Teaching by Television,* Council for Cultural Co-operation of the Council of Europe. Strasbourg A 65.

48   *How to make good pictures,* Kodak Ltd., London.

49   HUEBENER, T. *Audio-Visual Techniques in Teaching Foreign Languages,* New York University Press, 1960.

50   JOHNSON, F.C. and JOHNSON, L.A. and DYKSTRA, G. *Stick Figure Drawing for Language Teachers,* Ginn and Co. Ltd, The Jamaica Press, 1971.

51   KRACAUER, S. *Nature of Film,* Dobson, 1961.

52   *A Language Teaching Bibliography,* Comp. & Ed. by C.I.L.T. and E.T.I.C., Cambridge University Press.

53   LANCHESTER, W.S. *Hand Puppets and String Puppets,* Dryad.

54   LEE, W.R. *Language Teaching Games and Contests,* Oxford University Press.

55   LEE, W.R. and COPPEN, H. *Simple Audio-Visual Aids to Foreign Language Teaching,* O.U.P., 1964.

56   LEGGAT, R. *Showing Off or Display Techniques for the Teacher,* N.C.A.V.A.E., London, 1970.

57   LEWIS, *The Use of Diagrams in the Teaching of English,* Ginn & Co.

58   LIBBISH, B. ed. *Advances in the Teaching of Modern Languages,* Pergamon Press, 1964.

59   MACKAY, D. et al. *Breakthrough to Literacy, Teacher's Manual,* Longman for the Schools Council, 1970.

60   MACKEY, W.F. *Language Teaching Analysis,* Longman, 1965.

61   MIALARET, G. *The Psychology of the Use of Audio-Visual Aids in Primary Education,* Harrap/UNESCO.

62   MINOR and FRYE. *Techniques for Producing Visual Instructional Media,* McGraw-Hill, 1970.

63   MITTCHELL, F.J. *Practical Lettering and Layout,* A. & C. Black.

64   OLLERENSHAW, R. 'Design for Projection', *The Photographic Journal,* Feb. 1962.

65   *The Overhead Projector,* N.C.A.V.A.E., 1965.

66 POWELL, G.H. & POWELL L.S. *A Guide to the 8mm Loop Film,* B.A.C.I.E.

67 POWELL, L.S. *A Guide to the Overhead Projector,* B.A.C.I.E.,

68 REED, M.D. *Making Sound Filmstrips,* The Industrial Society, London, 1969.

69 ROWLANDS, D. *A Puppet Theatre for Language Teaching,* Materials Development Unit, Language Teaching Centre, University of York.

70 SCHULTZ, M.J. *The Teacher and Overhead Projection,* Prentice-Hall.

71 SEWELL, G.K. *Model Making in School,* N.C.A.V.A.E., London.

72 SPENCER, H. *The Visible World,* Lund Humphries, 1969.

73 *Sources of Information for Language Teachers in Britain,* C.I.L.T.

74 TANSEY P.J. and UNWIN D. *Simulation and Gaming in Education,* Methuen Education.

75 TAYLOR, E.A. *A Manual of Visual Presentation in Education & Training,* Pergamon Press.

76 UPTON, L.K. *Talk French,* Mary Glasgow Publications Ltd.

77 UPTON, L.K. 'Making full use of the Language Laboratory', *Visual Education.*

78 VALETTE, R. *Modern Language Testing: A Handbook,* Harcourt, Brace and World Inc., 1967.

79 *Veniss pamphlet-Audio Visual Teaching Materials for the Teaching of English as a Second Language,* N.C.A.V.A.E.

80 VENTNERS AND KING. *Répétitions,* Edward Arnold, 1969.

81 VERNON, M.D. *The Psychology of Perception,* Penguin Books, 1962.

82 WRIGHT, A. *Designing for Visual Aids,* Studio Vista, 1970.

83 WRIGHT, A. *Audio Visual Materials in Language Teaching,* Edinburgh Course in Applied Linguistics 3, Oxford University Press, 1974.

84 WRIGHT, A. 'The Role of the Artist in the Production of Visual Materials for Language Teaching,' in *Educational Sciences,* Vol. 1 No. 3, June 1967, Pergamon Press.

85 WRIGHT, A. 'Simple Drawing for Language Teaching', *Educational Development International* Vol 2 No. 3, July 1974.

86 WRIGHT, A. 'The Use of Pictures by Language Teachers', *Educational Development International,* Vol. 2 No. 4, September 1974.

87 YOUNG, J.B. *Reprographic Principles Made Easy,* N.C.A.V.A.E., 1970.

Appendices

I Sources of help and advice about language teaching materials and equipment

BRITISH COUNCIL EDUCATION AND SCIENCE DIVISION (A-V Department), Tavistock House South, Tavistock Square, London.

CENTRE FOR INFORMATION ON LANGUAGE TEACHING, The British Council, 10 Spring Gardens, London, S.W.1. (C.I.L.T.)

CENTRE FOR THE TEACHING OF READING, School of Education, University of Reading.

ENGLISH TEACHING INFORMATION CENTRE, 10 Spring Gardens, London S.W.1. (E.T.I.C.)

NATIONAL AUDIO-VISUAL AIDS CENTRE, 254-256 Belsize Road, London N.W.6. (N.C.A.V.A.E.)

THE EDUCATIONAL FOUNDATION FOR VISUAL AIDS, 33 Queen Anne Street, London W.1. (E.F.V.A.)

2 Sources of visual materials designed for language teaching

The publishers listed below are pleased to distribute their latest catalogue of the audio-visual materials on their current publishing list. For a detailed list of published materials refer to —

Audio-Visual Material for English Language Teaching; A Catalogue. Published by Longman, Burnt Mill, Harlow, Essex.

Audio-Visual Materials for Modern Language Teaching published by N.C.A.V.A.E. and E.F.V.A., 33 Queen Anne Street, London W.1. (Note yearly supplements available.)

ARNOLD, E.J. Butterley Street, Hunslet Lane, Leeds 10.

BBC PUBLICATIONS, 35 Marylebone High Street, London W.1.

BBC RADIO ENTERPRISES, P.O. Box 1AA London, W.1.

BBC TELEVISION ENTERPRISES, Educational and Training Film Sales Centre, London W.12.

CASSELL & COLLIER MACMILLAN LTD., 35 Red Lion Square, London, W.C.1.

COLLINS, WILLIAM, SONS & CO. LTD., 144 Cathedral Street, Glasgow.

EDUCATIONAL FOUNDATION FOR VISUAL AIDS, 33 Queen Anne Street, London W.1.

ENCYCLOPAEDIA BRITANNICA INTERNATIONAL LTD., Mappin House, 156-162 Oxford Street, London W.1.

ENGLISH UNIVERSITIES PRESS LTD., St. Paul's House, Warwick Lane, London E.C.1.

EUROPEAN SCHOOLBOOKS LTD., 122 Bath Road, Cheltenham, GL53 7JX.

GLASGOW, MARY BAKER LTD., 140 Kensington Church Street, London, W.8.

HARRAP G.G. & CO. LTD. and HARRAP AUDIO VISUAL AIDS, 182 High Holborn, London W.C.1.

INTERLANG LTD., 2 Clements Inn, London W.C.2.

LONGMAN GROUP LTD., Longman House, Burnt Mill, Harlow, Essex.

MACMILLAN EDUCATION, Houndmills, Basingstoke, Hants.

NATIONAL AUDIO-VISUAL AIDS LIBRARY, Paxton Place, Gipsy Road, London S.E.27.

NELSON, THOMAS & SON LTD., 36 Park Street, London W.1.

OLIVER & BOYD LTD., Croythorne House, 23 Ravelston Terrace, Edinburgh EH3 3TJ.

OXFORD UNIVERSITY PRESS, Ely House, 37 Dover Street, London, W.1.

PENGUIN BOOKS LTD., Bath Road, Harmondsworth, Mdx.

PERGAMON PRESS LTD., Headlington Hill Hall, Oxford.

TUTOR-TAPE CO. LTD., 2 Replingham Road, London S.W.18.

UNIVERSITY OF LONDON PRESS LTD., St. Paul's House, Warwick Lane, London E.C.4.

WARNE FREDRICK & CO. LTD., 40 Bedford Square, London W.C.1.

Publishers specialising in film and film strips for Language Teaching:

JAMES BRODIE, Brodie House, 15 Queen Square, Bath, Somerset.

CAMERA TALKS LTD., 31 North Row, Park Lane, London W.1.

COMMON GROUND, Longman Group, Longman House, Burnt Mill, Harlow, Essex.

EDUCATIONAL PRODUCTIONS, East Ardsley, Wakefield, Yorks.

ENCYCLOPAEDIA BRITANNICA FILMSTRIPS, Educational Division, Dorland House, 18-20 Lower Regent Street, London S.W.1.

RANK FILM LIBRARY, 1 Aintree Road, Perivale, Mdx.

SOUND SERVICES, Instructional Aids Department, Kingston Road, Merton Park, London S.W.19.

3   Sources of visual material not specifically designed for language teaching

The Organisations listed below offer visual materials either free of charge or at reasonable prices. Although these materials are not intended for language teaching they *are* intended for study, for reading and to promote discussion. The July issue of *Visual Education* lists a great number of such organisations. Other sources include official representatives of the target country, for example, the British Council for Britain, or the Goethe Institute for Germany; also organisations representing travel and trade.

ALUMINIUM FEDERATION, Broadway House, 60 Calthorpe Road, Five Ways, Birmingham, B15 1TN.

AUSTRALIA NEWS AND INFORMATION BUREAU, Canberra House, 10-16 Maltravers Street, Strand, London W.C.2.

BIRDS EYE FOODS LTD., Educational Service, Station Avenue, Walton-on-Thames, Surrey.

BOWATER PAPER CORPORATION LTD., Bowater House, Knightsbridge, London S.W.1.

BRITISH ATLANTIC COMMITTEE, Benjamin Franklin House, 36 Craven Street, London, W.C.1.

BRITISH MAN-MADE FIBRES FEDERATION, 41 Dover Street, London W.1.

BRITISH STEEL CORPORATION, Information Office, 33 Grosvenor Place, London S.W.1.

BROOKE BOND OXO EDUCATION SERVICE, Leon House, High Street, Croydon, CR9 1JQ.

CADBURY SCHWEPPES LTD., Schools Department, Bournville, Birmingham.

CENTRAL OFFICE OF INFORMATION, Hercules Road, Westminster Bridge Road, London, S.E.1.

CEYLON TEA CENTRE, Education Department, 22 Regent Street, London S.W.1.

COMMONWEALTH INSTITUTE, Kensington High Street, London W.8

COUNTRYSIDE COMMISSION, 1 Cambridge Gate, Regent's Park, London N.W.1.

DUNLOP LTD., Dunlop House, Ryder Street, St. James's, London S.W.1.

EDUCATIONAL PRODUCTIONS LTD., East Ardsley, Wakefield, Yorkshire.

ELECTRICITY COUNCIL, 30 Millbank, London S.W.1.

EUROPEAN COMMUNITY INFORMATION OFFICE, 23 Chesham Street, London S.W.1.

FORESTRY COMMISSION, 25 Savile Row, London, W1X 2AY.

GENERAL DENTAL COUNCIL, 37 Wimpole Street, London, W1M 8DQ.

GERBER BABY COUNCIL, Claygate House, Esher, Surrey.

H.J. HEINZ CO. LTD., Hayes Park, Hayes, Middlesex.

HEINZ HOME COOKERY SERVICE, Greater London House, Hampstead Road, London N.W.1.

HER MAJESTY'S STATIONERY OFFICE, P.O. Box 569, London S.E.1.

ICI FIBRES LTD., Publicity Department, 68 Knightsbridge, London S.W.1.

ISLE OF MAN TOURIST BOARD, 13 Victoria Street, Douglas, Isle of Man.

KEEP BRITAIN TIDY GROUP, 76/86 Strand, London W.C.2.

LEVER BROTHERS LTD., Education Unit, Lever House, 21/23 New Fetter Lane, London E.C.4.

LONDON TRANSPORT, Publicity Office, Griffith House, 280 Old Marylebone Road, London N.W.1.

NATIONAL COAL BOARD, Public Relations, Hobart House, Grosvenor Place, London S.W.1.

NATIONAL GALLERY ' Trafalgar Square, London W.C.2.

NATIONAL MONUMENTS RECORD, Fielden House, 10 Great College Street, London S.W.2.

NATIONAL PORTRAIT GALLERY, London W.C.2.

NATIONAL SAVINGS COMMITTEE, Alexandra House, Kingsway, London WC2B 6TS.

NORTHERN IRELAND GOVERNMENT OFFICE, Stormont Castle, Belfast, BT4 3ST.

PORT OF LONDON AUTHORITY, Public Relations Officer, Trinity Square, P.O. Box 242, London E.C.3.

POTATO MARKETING BOARD, 50 Hans Crescent, London S.W.1.

RICE COUNCIL, 87 Notting Hill Gate, London W.11.

ROYAL SOCIETY FOR THE PREVENTION OF CRUELTY TO ANIMALS, The Manor House, Horsham, Sussex RH12 1HG.

SHELL INTERNATIONAL PETROLEUM CO. LTD., Shell Centre, London S.E.1.

THE COTTON BOARD, 3 Alberton Street, Manchester 3.

THE NESTLE CO. LTD., St. George's House, Croydon, Surrey, CR9 1NR.

THE ROYAL SOCIETY FOR THE PREVENTION OF ACCIDENTS, Royal Oak Centre, Brighton Road, Purley CR2 2UR.

UNILEVER, Education Section, Unilever House, Blackfriars, London E.C.4.

UNITED NATIONS INFORMATION CENTRE, 14/15 Stratford Place, London W.1.

VAN DEN BERGHS LTD., Public Relations Department, Kildare House, Dorset Rise, London S.W.1.

VICTORIA AND ALBERT MUSEUM, London S.W.7.

YOUTH HOSTELS ASSOCIATION, Trevelyan House, St. Albans, Herts.

The journal, *Movie Maker* prints, annually, a guide to sponsored films as a section in one of its monthly issues. The films are on many different subjects and may be used in a variety of ways by the language teacher. Many of these films are first class technically and most are lent free of charge. Only a very few of the addresses supplied by *Movie Maker are* listed below. It would be advisable for those interested to write to *Movie Maker* and ask for their latest guide. (*Movie Maker* 46-47 Chancery Lane, London W.C.2.)

AUSTRALIAN INFORMATION BUREAU, Canberra House, Maltravers Street, Strand, London W.C.2.

BERGEN LINE PUBLICITY DEPARTMENT, Norway House, 21/24 Cockspur Street, London S.W.1.

BRITISH AIRCRAFT CORPORATION, Cranford Lane, Heston,

BRITISH STEEL CORPORATION, Exhibition and Films Department, Park House, 118 Park Street, London, W1Y 4BO.

BRITISH TRANSPORT FILM LIBRARY, Melbury House, Melbury Terrace, London N.W.1.

CENTRAL FILM LIBRARY, Government Building, Bromyard Avenue, London W.3.

COCA-COLA EXPORT CORPORATION, Atlantic House, 7 Rockley Road, London, W14 0DH.

DUNLOP FILM LIBRARY, 269 Kingston Road, Merton Park, London S.W.19.

ICI FILM LIBRARY, Thames House, North Millbank, London S.W.1.

NATIONAL AUDIO VISUAL AIDS LIBRARY, 2 Paxton Place, Gipsy Road, London S.E.2.

RANK FILM LIBRARY, P.O. Box 70, Great West Road, Brentford, Middlesex.

SOUND-SERVICES LTD., 269 Kingston Road, Merton Park, London S.W.19.

4   Sources of materials for the manufacture of visuals

The suppliers listed below distribute goods in Britain. It is not in the main profitable for the suppliers to send materials out of the country.

ARNOLD, E.J. & SON LTD., Butterley Street, Leeds 10.

BOSTIK LTD., Leicester.

DRYAD HANDICRAFTS, 22 Bloomsbury Street, London W.C.1.

EDUCATIONAL SUPPLY ASSOCIATION (ESA), Pinnacles, Harlow, Essex.

MATTHEWS DREW & SHELBOURNE LTD., 78 High Holborn, London W.C.2.

PHILIP & TACEY LTD., North Way, Walworth Industrial Estate, Andover, Hants.

REEVES & SONS LTD., Lincoln Road, Enfield, Middlesex.

ROWNEY, GEORGE & CO. LTD., P.O. Box 10, Bracknell, Berkshire.

WINSOR & NEWTON LTD., Whitefriars Drive, Wealdstone, Harrow, Middlesex.